Black Americans
From Africa to the 80's
Reading Comprehension
⌐ Vol. I ⌐
Table of Contents

This book
was purchased by the
Allen County Public Library
Foundation
with funds donated
by library supporters
to match a
National Endowment for
the Humanities
challenge grant for the
purchase of books
in the humanities
fields.

A Question to Think About Before We Start

Who is a "Black American?"

The "American" part is easy. An American is anyone who lives in America or thinks of America as his or her home. ("America" means all the countries of North and South America, but in this book we use it to mean only the United States.)

The "Black" part is not so easy. Have you ever seen anyone who was truly "black" in color? Or "white?" Americans may be of any shade from very dark to very light—lighter than many "white" people. Probably the darkest-skinned people in the world are the Dravidian people of India. Some Dravidians live in the United States—but would we call them "Black Americans?"

You can see the problems you run into when you try to label other people according to their skin color—or their religion or national group, for that matter. It leads some people to a belief that a person's character, abilities, and value as a human being can be a matter of race. From there it's all too easy to start believing that one race of people can be said to be better than another. This way of thinking has a name: *racism.*

In one way, this book is the story of Black Americans' 400-year struggle against racism.

Let's get back to our first question: who is a Black American?

Black Americans are one of many groups of people who share in the heritage and culture of all Americans but who have also given America something of their own special heritage and culture. All of these groups, even the Indians, came from someplace else. For Black Americans, that "someplace" is the continent of Africa.

You notice that we still haven't answered the question. When you're talking about 25 million people, there's no quick and easy way to answer a question like that. No matter what definition you come up with, a lot of people are going to be left out. We'll leave it up to you to answer the question "Who is a Black American?" when you've finished reading this book.

A Few Words About Names

At different times during our history, people have used other names to refer to Black Americans—"Negroes," "persons of color," "colored people," and other, less polite names. Because a lot of this book is about earlier times and we're trying to tell things as they were, you'll find some of these names here. Most of them are now considered a little insulting by Black Americans, but they weren't always thought of that way. (In fact, before 1966, most "American Negroes" would have been terribly offended if someone called them "black!")

You'll read about many such changes in this book, starting with the next page.

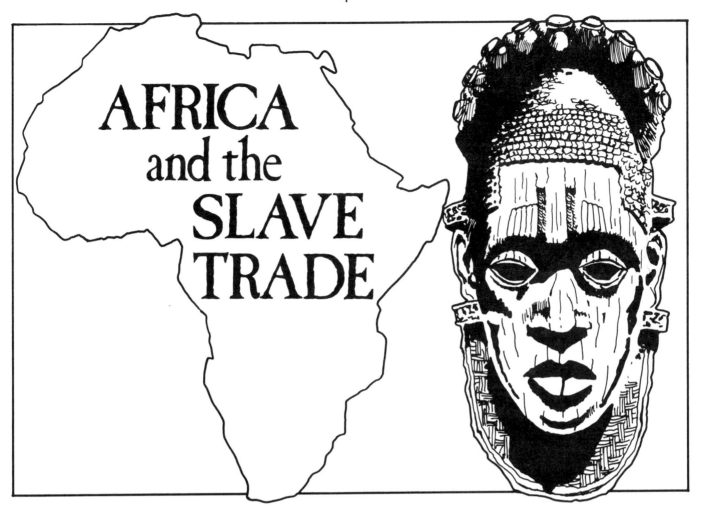

Chapter 1

AFRICA and the SLAVE TRADE

The story of Black Americans begins in Africa. Of course, there is no one group of people in Africa of which we can say, "These people were the ancestors of Black Americans." Africa is the second largest continent on Earth. It is four times the size of the United States. The Africans who came to America were of many different nations and tribes. They followed different ways of life and spoke hundreds of different languages. (Even today, there are more than 200 languages spoken in the country of Nigeria alone.) Some of these African nations and tribes numbered thousands of people. Others consisted of only a few families.

We do know that most of the Africans who were brought to America came from the western part of Africa. Looking closer, we can say that most of them came from the area near the seacoast, from the Senegal River in the north, down around the huge "bulge" to the country known today as Angola. That's a 3,000-mile length of seacoast. But other people came from the interi-or of West Africa, from the *sudan,* or grasslands, south of the great Sahara Desert. And still others came from East Africa, from Mozambique and the island of Madagascar.

People of the western and coastal regions, such as the Ashanti, Mandingo, Hausa, Ibo, Wolof, and Yoruba tribes, were usually tall with broad features, woolly hair, and a skin color of almost true black. The Bantu peoples, who lived farther east and south, were more brown than black. And the people of Madagascar resembled their distant cousins in Southeast Asia and the far-off islands of the Pacific Ocean. The Africans brought to America included the Nilotics, the tallest people in the world, and the Congo Pygmies, among the shortest. When you realize that nearly all Black Americans also include Europeans and American Indians among their ancestors, you can see how silly it is to talk about a black "race!"

Africa was home to many different cultures. Some African peoples were nomads who lived by

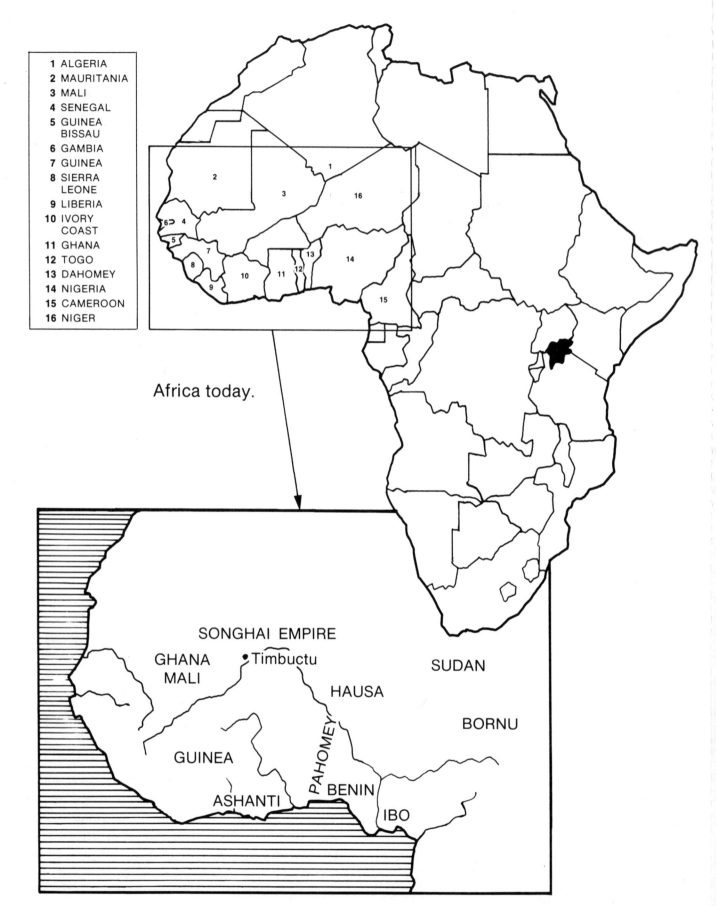

1 ALGERIA
2 MAURITANIA
3 MALI
4 SENEGAL
5 GUINEA BISSAU
6 GAMBIA
7 GUINEA
8 SIERRA LEONE
9 LIBERIA
10 IVORY COAST
11 GHANA
12 TOGO
13 DAHOMEY
14 NIGERIA
15 CAMEROON
16 NIGER

Africa today.

Some historic nations of West Africa's past.

hunting and gathering. Others were farmers, growing wheat, rice, cotton, and various fruits and vegetables. Others herded goats and cattle. Still others lived in cities and practiced a variety of trades and professions. It was probably in West Africa that people first discovered how to make iron. The art of Africa, in metal, wood, stone, cloth, and ivory, can be seen and admired in museums around the world. Some of the greatest artists of Europe and America borrowed ideas for their paintings from the arts of Africa. The music of Africa, too, can be heard in many borrowed forms all over the world.

Though most African peoples followed the ancient religions of their tribes, there were many Muslims among them, and in some regions, Christians and Jews as well. Very often the king and ruling family would be Muslims while the common people would follow the old religion.

All of these people—kings, queens and nobles, hunters and farmers, builders and artisans, scholars and warriors—were among the ancestors of Black Americans.

In some parts of the Americas, such as Brazil and the islands of the West Indies, black people still speak African languages and follow some of the old African customs. But in the United States, the years of slavery nearly wiped out any memories of Africa. Only in the Sea Islands, off the coast of Georgia and South Carolina, can you hear words of African languages mixed in with the English. And some Black Americans might remember hearing "Aunt Nancy tales" from their grandmothers. "Aunt Nancy" is an American version of "Anansi," a trick-playing spider character from West African folklore.

West African History: A Few Highlights

Until the last hundred years or so, Africa's long and colorful history remained pretty much unknown to Europeans and Americans. People knew about the great civilizations of Egypt and the extreme northern part of Africa, but the rest of the continent was a mystery.

Take a look at the two maps on page 6. The first is a map of Africa today, while the second shows the location of some of the historic kingdoms of the past. You may notice that some of the names are the same—but are in different places. The modern West African nations of Ghana and Mali are named in honor of great African empires that flourished long ago.

The original Ghana was a powerful kingdom in West Africa as early as the year 500. You can still see the ruins of its capital, Kumbi Saleh, in the modern nation of Mauretania. Ghana became a wealthy nation because of gold and ivory. Most of the gold brought to Europe and the Middle East during the Middle Ages came from the mines of Ghana, carried across the desert by camel caravan.

Ghana was at the height of its power in the year 1067, when an Arab traveler named Al Bekri visited there. Here is what he reported:

The king of Ghana is named Tenkaminen. He is the master of a large empire and a formidable power. The king can put 200,000 warriors in the field, more than 40,000 armed with bows and arrows. . . .

When he gives audience to his people, to hear their complaints and do justice, he sits in a large tent around which stand ten servants holding shields and gold-handled swords. On his right are the sons of the princes of his empire, splendidly dressed, and with gold plaited into their hair. The leaders of the government sit on the ground all around the king. The gate of the king's chamber is guarded by dogs who wear gold and silver collars. . . .

The best gold in Ghana comes from a town about 18 days' journey from the capital, in a country that is densely populated and covered with villages. All the pieces of gold found in the mines of the empire belong to the king, but he lets the public keep the gold dust. The people of this region are traders, and they carry gold dust all over the place.

Soon after Al Bekri's visit, Ghana was invaded by fierce Muslim warriors from northern Africa. Kumbi Saleh was captured and burned. Ghana never fully recovered from this defeat.

The empire of Mali was ruled by the Mandingo tribe. Mandingoes today still tell the story of Sundiata, the slave boy who rose to become the first emperor of Mali. At the height of its power, in the 1300s, Mali stretched across western Africa from Senegal to the borders of Nigeria. Mali's greatest emperor was Mansa Musa ("King Moses") who ruled from 1312 to 1337. He built the cities of Timbuktu and Gao into great trading centers. He invited scholars from Egypt to help

The king of Ghana gives an audience.

set up a university in Timbuktu.

Mansa Musa was a Muslim, and in 1324 he left Mali for a pilgrimage to Mecca, the Muslim holy city (now in Saudi Arabia). Mansa Musa's trip lasted two years. In Egypt, where he stopped for several months, the people talked about his visit for years afterward. He and his court gave away so much gold as presents to the Egyptians that "it ruined the value of money!" Largely because of Mansa Musa's power and wealth, Mali remained the most important nation in Africa until about 1400.

Other civilizations and kingdoms rose and fell in different parts of West Africa at different times. Some, like Ghana and Mali, lasted for centuries. Others did not survive long past the lifetime of a single powerful king. Some of these kingdoms fell to invaders from the Sahara Desert and from North Africa. More often, they were defeated by an enemy that still troubles West Africa today: drought. But by 1500 a new enemy had appeared in Africa: slave traders from Europe.

The Slave Trade

Slavery—people owning other people as property—is as old as human history. Only in the last 200 years or so have people come to recognize slavery as an evil. Yet even today slavery exists in some parts of the world. People have been made slaves by being captured in war, as punishment for crimes, for failure to pay debts— or simply because the people of one nation felt themselves to be "more human" than those of another, and they had the power to enslave. People of nearly every nation on earth have been slaves at one time or another. People of nearly every nation have been slave owners, too.

In Africa, as in other places, slavery was a part of social and economic life. The law said that slaves were property, but some slaves became trusted members of the master's family and lived almost as free people. Others, however, were sold to slave traders and taken out of the country. In most parts of Africa, as in other parts of the world, slavery was not necessarily forever. Slaves were often given their freedom. The children born to slaves could not be sold away from their parents. A one-time slave or the child of a slave could rise to a high position.

But when Europeans began trading for slaves

After capture by slave traders, Africans were marched to the coast in chains.

in Africa, the Africans unlucky enough to be sold found themselves in a different sort of slavery. Many Europeans looked upon black skin as a mark of inferiority. They saw no reason to treat Africans as human beings. An African slave was in most cases to be permanently a slave.

The African slave trade began even before Columbus discovered America. In 1441, a young Portuguese ship captain, Antonio Gonsalves, sailed to the west coast of Africa to buy animal hides and oil. He brought back ten African slaves as presents for Prince Henry of Portugal.

Most of the major sea-going nations of Europe traded in Africa. Besides animal skins and oil, gold and ivory were an important part of the cargo. But after the discovery of America, human beings became the most important of Africa's "trade goods." The Europeans needed many slaves to work on their *plantations* (large farms) and in their mines in the "New World." By the 1600s, England, Portugal, Holland, Spain, Denmark, Sweden, and Germany were all actively involved in the slave trade. Between 1441 and the time the West African slave trade ended in the 1800s, perhaps 25 million Africans were carried away as slaves.

When a European trader landed on the African coast, he set up a fort and a trading station. Rarely did Europeans go into the interior to capture slaves. Usually they stayed on the coast and bought slaves from other Africans. Eager to trade for guns, iron tools, liquor, and other European goods, one tribe would raid another.

They seized whatever captives they could and marched them in chains to the trading stations on the coast.

Usually the trader began by offering presents to the native king. Then the bargaining got under way. Prices varied greatly, but the average cost of a healthy male was about $60 in goods (worth eight to ten times as much today). A woman could be bought for $45. Finally, the trader took the precaution of having the slaves examined by a doctor.

What happened to Africans who were captured for the slave trade? We're going to let two people to whom it actually happened tell their own stories, one of being captured, the other of the voyage to America on a slave ship. (We've simplified their words somewhat.)

The first story was told by an elderly man named Venture Smith in 1795. Venture had been captured as a child, and sold as a slave in America. His last master had allowed him to work for himself by evening in order to buy his freedom. When he wrote this story, Venture had been a free man in Connecticut for many years.

I was born at Dukandarra, in Guinea, about the year 1729. My father had three wives. Every man was allowed to have as many wives as he could afford to maintain. I was the oldest of the three children of my father's first wife, and my name was Broteer.

The first important thing I remember was a quarrel between my father and mother. He had married his third wife without her consent, which was against the custom of our people. My mother then left my father and traveled away with her three children to the east. I was then five years old. [*Venture goes on to tell about his dangerous journey and his experience working as a shepherd for a rich farmer. After a year, his parents made up, and he returned to live with his father.*]

No more than six weeks had passed after my return before a messenger came from the place where I had spent the past year. He said that an army from a nearby nation had invaded, paid and equipped by some white nation to conquer the country. His people had lived for so long in peace that they were not prepared for war and could not defend themselves. [*Venture describes how his father agreed to allow these people to stay in his country. The invaders destroyed the neighboring kingdom and threatened to conquer Venture's people too, if his father did not pay them a large sum of money and animals as tribute. Venture's father went along with these demands, and the invaders promised not to attack them. But the invaders did not intend to keep their promise. Venture describes the attack by the enemy and the courage shown by his father in defending himself.*]

The enemy found us hiding in the reeds, and the first greeting I had from them was a blow on the back of the head with the barrel of a gun, and at the same time a grasp around the neck. I had a rope put around my neck, as had all the women with me. We were led to my father who was likewise tied up. We were led to the enemy's camp. The women and myself were not treated too badly. But my father was tortured in order to make him tell where his money was hidden. I watched while he was tortured to death. The shocking scene is still fresh in my mind, and I have often been overcome when thinking about it. . . .

The enemy's army was large, consisting of about 6,000 men. After they killed my father, they broke camp and immediately began marching to the sea, taking us as prisoners. The enemy had remarkable success in destroying the country wherever they went. They burned the villages and captured the people. The distance they brought us was 400 miles. [*At the end of the journey to the sea, Venture was put aboard a sailing ship bound for Rhode Island, along with 260 other prisoners.*]

This second story was told by a man named Olaudah Equiano, who was born in what is now Nigeria. Olaudah was sold into slavery as a boy in 1756, and spent ten years as a slave in America. After he bought his freedom, he went to England. He spent the rest of his life fighting slavery and helping freed slaves return to Africa. He wrote this terrifying story of the "middle passage" in 1791.

A slave trader forces his captives to exercise.

The first thing I saw when I arrived on the coast was the sea, where a slave ship was waiting for its cargo. I was terrified when I was carried on board. I was sure I had got into a world of bad spirits who were going to kill me. They looked so different from us with their white skin and long hair. When I looked around the ship, I saw a huge furnace boiling, and many black people chained together. Every one of their faces showed grief and sorrow. I was sure now that my worst fears were true. Some of the black people who had brought us on board were nearby to receive their pay. I asked if we were going to be eaten by these white men with horrible looks, red faces, and long hair. They told me that we would not. Soon afterward, these men went ashore, and I was left alone with my grief and fear.

Soon I was put under the decks. I was immediately greeted by the most horrible smell I have ever experienced in my life. I became so sick and low in spirit that I was not able to eat anything. Nor did I want to. I wanted only to die. But when I refused to eat, two of the white men tied me down and whipped me, and then forced me to eat.

After a while, I found among the poor chained men one of my own country who spoke my language. He told me that we were not going to be eaten, but that we were being brought to the white men's country to work for them. Still I feared that I would be killed, because I had never seen any people act with such brutal cruelty—not only to us blacks, but to their own kind as well. Once, when I was allowed on deck, I saw a man of the crew flogged so brutally that he died of it. Then they threw him over the side as if he were an animal. . . .

When the ship had her full cargo, we were all forced below decks. While we were on the coast, the stench of the hold was unbear-ably disgusting, but at least we were sometimes allowed on deck. But now that the hold was full and the ship was on the sea, it was more horrible than can be imagined. We were chained so close together that each of us hardly had enough room to turn in. It was so hot and so crowded and everyone perspired so much that breathing was almost impossible. There was also the stench of the tubs used for toilets, which children sometimes fell into. The chains cut into people's skin. Many people became sick and died. . . .

I was luckier than many. Anyone who looked close to death was brought on deck for fresh air, and I was on deck more than most of the others. In fact, I wished that I would die, and gain my freedom this way. One day, three of my countrymen managed to jump off the ship into the sea. The sailors went after them in a small boat. Two of them had drowned, and the third was beaten mercilessly for preferring death to slavery. . . .

[Olaudah goes on to describe more of the horrors of the voyage. He also tells of his curiosity about how the ship was made to move and how the sailors could steer it. When the ship reaches land, he and the other prisoners are herded into pens and sold to their new masters. Olaudah ends his story with a plea that the world put an end to slavery.]

Questions and Activities for Chapter 1

Name _____ Date _____

I. UNDERSTANDING THE WORDS

Circle the letter of the answer that means the same as the underlined word in each sentence. Use a dictionary if you need help.

1. The ancestors of Black Americans came from Africa.
   - a) earlier generations
   - b) art and music
   - c) descendants

2. Africa is the second largest continent on earth.
   - a) country
   - b) race
   - c) large land mass

3. Africa was home to many different cultures.
   - a) wild animals
   - b) people's beliefs, customs, and art
   - c) kinds of music

4. People in West Africa included hunters and farmers, builders and artisans.
   - a) slave traders
   - b) tax collectors
   - c) people skilled at a craft

5. The king of ancient Ghana was a formidable power.
   - a) strong
   - b) very formal
   - c) negligible

6. Mansa Musa set up a university in Timbuktu.
   - a) fortress
   - b) school for training soldiers
   - c) school for advanced study

7. Mansa Musa made a great pilgrimage to Mecca.
   - a) sea voyage
   - b) religious journey
   - c) gift of money

8. Drought still plagues West Africa today.
   - a) European slave traders
   - b) religious war
   - c) long periods without rain

9. European traders seized their black captives and forced them aboard ships.
   - a) captured
   - b) ignored
   - c) mistreated

10. In Africa, slavery was a part of social and economic life.
    - a) relations among people
    - b) education
    - c) mathematics

11. In the sentence above, economic has to do with
    - a) sports and entertainment.
    - b) religion.
    - c) money, property, and business.

12. In the days of the slave trade, many Europeans looked upon black skin as a mark of inferiority.
    - a) great courage
    - b) being of less worth
    - c) disease

II. UNDERSTANDING THE FACTS

Circle T if the sentence is true. Circle F if the sentence is false.

T F 1. Africa is the second largest country on earth.

T F 2. The ancestors of most Black Americans came from the southern part of Africa.

T F 3. The Nilotic people of Africa are the tallest people in the world.

T F 4. Most African peoples in the 1500s lived by hunting.

T F 5. Many Africans believed in the Muslim religion.

T F 6. Black Americans in many parts of the United States speak African languages along with English.

T F 7. Kumbi Saleh was the ancient capital of Mauretania.

T F 8. Ancient Ghana became a wealthy nation because of gold and ivory.

T F 9. Ancient Ghana was not in the same place as modern Ghana.

T F 10. Sundiata was a slave boy who became emperor of Mali.

T F 11. Mansa Musa had little use for scholars or learning.

T F 12. Mansa Musa made a famous journey to Jerusalem.

T F 13. Before 1400 there had never been slavery in Africa.

T F 14. About 25 million Africans were carried away as slaves.

T F 15. White slave traders often went deep into Africa to capture slaves.

T F 16. Venture Smith was sold into slavery when he was 20 years old.

T F 17. Among Venture's people, a man could have more than one wife.

T F 18. Olaudah Equiano was born in Ghana.

T F 19. Olaudah was afraid he was going to be eaten by the slave traders.

T F 20. Olaudah bought his freedom after being a slave for ten years.

III. THOUGHTS OF YOUR OWN

Use a separate sheet of paper to answer these questions.

1. Why would modern African nations take the names of ancient kingdoms that did not occupy the same land?

2. Why do you think some Africans so readily helped Europeans capture other Africans for slavery? Do you think people in our country would do the same thing if we were invaded by a stronger, foreign enemy? Why or why not?

3. Why do you think Europeans felt that they had the right to enslave Africans?

4. You're an African, growing up at the time of the slave trade. How is your life affected by knowing that you could be kidnapped by slave traders? Since the people taken away don't come back, what do you think happens to them?

IV. FOR FAST WORKERS

Learn more about Africa! Use your school or public library to find the information, then write a one- or two-page report on one of the following subjects:

A. One of the nations or tribes in Africa from which Black Americans are descended. Find out how they lived during the days of the slave trade and how and where they live today. The names of some of the nations and tribes are: Ashanti, Wolof (Jolof), Mandingo (Mandinka), Ibo, Hausa, Yoruba, Fante, and Fulani.

B. One of the nations of modern West Africa.

C. African art or music.

Chapter 2

THE YEARS of SLAVERY

On an August day in 1619, a Dutch ship left 20 Africans on the dock in Jamestown, Virginia. These 17 men and three women were the first Black Americans.

These first Black Americans were not slaves. They were *indentured servants.* That meant that they had *indentures,* or *contracts,* that bound them to work for their masters for a set length of time—usually four years. At the end of that time, the master had to give them "freedom dues"—clothes, money, or a piece of land.

Indentured servants, both black and white, were common in England and in England's American colonies. People became bound as payment for the cost of their transportation to America, as payment for debt, or as punishment for a crime. But in 1662, a law was passed saying that only white people could be indentured servants. Black servants were forced into permanent slavery. By 1700, there were slaves in every one of England's American colonies.

Slavery in America was very different than indentured servitude. Slaves were recognized as property, like a piece of land or a horse. A slave was a slave for life. By bearing children, the slaves increased the master's property, since the children belonged to the master as well.

From the beginning, slavery took hold more strongly in the South than in the North. Most slaves were put to work on the large plantations where tobacco, rice, sugar cane, and indigo were grown. These crops did not grow well in the North. Many workers were needed to clear the land for these crops and to plant and harvest them, so there was always a demand for new slaves from Africa. There were far fewer slaves in the North than in the South. It also was easier for a northern slave to do extra work and to buy his or her freedom after a few years. Some freed slaves even owned slaves themselves! In the North more white people were opposed to slavery, and slaves were better treated than in the South. But a slave, North or South, was still a slave—still the property of his or her master. Even though slavery was unpopular in the North, many northerners were making money from it. Nearly all the ships that carried slaves from Africa were owned by northern merchants.

How hard were slaves worked on the plantations of the South? In the 1760s the colony of South Carolina found it necessary to pass a strict law regulating the treatment of slaves by masters. It was forbidden to work slaves more than 15 hours a day in the spring and summer or more than 14 hours a day in the fall and winter. This law was not passed out of kindness to the slaves. The owners were warned not to treat slaves so cruelly that they might revolt against their masters.

Black Americans in the Revolutionary War

The war for independence from England made many white Americans think about the slave system. If this is a fight for freedom, people reasoned, shouldn't there be freedom for all? Most northerners were opposed to slavery, and even many southerners had their doubts. In March, 1770, there was a riot in Boston that became known as the Boston Massacre. A group of young men began taunting a young British soldier and throwing snowballs at him. Other soldiers arrived to help him. A free-for-all followed, with the crowd throwing anything they could find at the soldiers. Finally, shots were fired. Three Bostonians were killed instantly, and two others died later from their wounds. The incident outraged Americans in all the colonies.

Among the men killed in the first volley of shots was Crispus Attucks. He was a runaway slave who had been living as a free man for 20 years, working as a sailor and a shipyard worker. History has recorded his name as the man "first to fall" in America's struggle for freedom.

It is a little hard now to look on Crispus Attucks as a hero. Witnesses agreed that he had been hitting a British soldier with a heavy club before the shots were fired. But some colonists remarked on the fact that the person who was first to die in their struggle for freedom was a man who was not as free as they.

When the fighting began, there were many people who were against arming Black Americans

Crispus Attucks

to fight the British. In the South especially but also in the North, people were afraid of putting guns in the hands of black men. Thomas Jefferson had tried to write a strong anti-slavery message into the Declaration of Independence, even though he was a slave owner himself. But too many people were against the idea, and that section was cut out of the Declaration before it was signed. But the leaders of the new American nation began to encourage black soldiers to join the army after the British promised freedom to any slave who would join their side!

About 5,000 Black Americans, some slaves and some free, fought for independence. Some became heroes of the revolution. Salem Poor, a free man from Massachusetts, fired the shot that killed one of the British commanders at the famous battle of Bunker Hill. There were all-black units in the Continental Army, some of which served under black officers. Mark Starlin, a Black American from Virginia, was captain of a ship in the American Navy. After the war, Captain Starlin was forced back into slavery by his old master. But many Black Americans used the confusion of the war to escape to freedom.

Cotton Becomes King

Independence for the new United States meant the beginning of the end of slavery in the North. Some of the northern states had passed laws putting an end to slavery before the war ended. Others followed within a few years. Even in the South many felt that slavery was a "necessary evil." But southerners had a great deal of money invested in their "property," and people easily become angry at the idea of someone trying to take their property away from them. To speak out against slavery in the South was becoming more and more dangerous.

Eli Whitney's cotton gin changed the economy of the South.

Then in 1793, an inventor named Eli Whitney invented a machine called a *cotton gin.* This machine made it easy to separate seeds from cotton fiber. Suddenly, cotton became a tremendously valuable crop to anyone with the right kind of land for growing it—the kind of land found in the deep South. Owners of cotton plantations could become rich quickly. Poor people with a small parcel of land and a slave or two to work it could become prosperous farmers. As the United States expanded westward between 1800 and 1830, so did the "cotton kingdom" of the South—and so did slavery. Cotton plantations became the basis of the South's economy, and cotton plantations ran on slave labor.

White southerners' attitudes toward slavery changed as cotton became more important. While in 1790 slavery was looked upon as a "necessary evil," by 1820 it was seen as a "positive good"—good for the masters, good for the slaves. By 1850, white southerners were saying that "God had intended" for whites to be masters and blacks to be slaves.

Slaves and Masters

Every southern city and town had its slave

At a slave market, people were bought and sold at auction.

market where slaves were bought and sold. A strong, young slave could be worth as much as $1,500 (more than $12,000 in today's money). The value of a slave depended upon his or her age, strength, special skills, and ability to produce children. This became especially important after 1808, when it became illegal to bring in new slaves from Africa. (Legal or not, slave ships continued to bring their human cargoes to southern ports.)

In most southern states, there were laws that prevented a master from killing a slave "without cause." Otherwise a slave had no rights. A slave

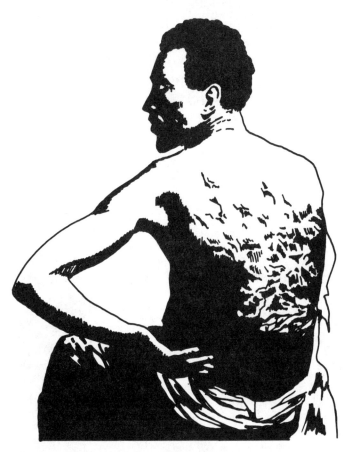

Many slaves bore the scars of whips on their backs.
(from an old photograph)

could be whipped or beaten for such "crimes" as trying to run away, not working as hard as a master wished, or even talking back to a white person. More serious crimes meant branding, imprisonment, or death. And if a master killed a slave, it was rarely looked on as murder.

Not all slave owners were cruel. The kinder masters did not allow their slaves to be mistreated and made certain that they were well fed and clothed. Other masters, while they hardly thought of their slaves as human beings, wanted to protect their property. But while many masters did not "rule by the whip," all ruled by the threat of the whip.

Different states had their own "slave codes," as the laws concerning slavery were called. But the point of all of them was that slaves were not people but *property,* and the laws were meant to protect the owner's property. Slaves could not leave their masters' land without a written pass. They could not visit the homes of whites or free blacks. They could not hold meetings without a white person being present, except (in some states) for church services. In most southern states, it was against the law for a slave to go to church or for a master to teach a slave to read or write. This was a law that was often broken. Still, many slaveowners feared that education and religion might give their slaves "dangerous ideas"—such as the wish for freedom.

Some states even had laws saying that slaves could not marry. But most slaves did marry and stay together in families. There was always the danger that a master would break up a family by selling off one or more of its members. Most masters recognized that this was terribly cruel. But that didn't always keep them from selling a slave away from his or her family if they needed the cash. Often a slave would be sold as punishment for running away.

Slavery:
On the Plantations and In the Cities

On the cotton and tobacco plantations of the South, and on the large farms where other crops were grown, all the work was done by slaves. The largest plantations were worked by hundreds of slaves, but most plantations in the South had fewer than 20 slaves. Some white farmers might own just one or two slaves, while the great majority of white southerners were not slave-owners at all.

On the plantations, most of the slaves were field hands. They worked in the cotton fields "from day clean to first dark" in large gangs watched over by an *overseer.* The overseer was the most hated man on the plantation. It was his job to see that the slaves kept working and to discipline them—usually with a whip.

Field hands usually lived in small cabins with dirt floors and no windows. They ate cornmeal

Slave quarters on a plantation.

and sweet potatoes, and sometimes a bit of fish or meat. On some plantations, slaves were allowed to raise vegetables and chickens and to hunt for food in whatever spare time they could find. There usually wasn't much: a field hand worked from Monday through Saturday, and sometimes part of Sunday, too.

A slave with a valuable skill might have special privileges. Some slaves worked as carpenters, mechanics, blacksmiths, cooks, wagon drivers, and house servants. The house servants might live in the master's house and wear his family's cast-off clothing. But they were slaves every bit as much as were the field hands. Some slaves who had special skills might be hired out by their masters to work on other plantations for a day to a week or more. Some were talented musicians whose masters would hire them out to play at parties on other plantations or in cities. A few slave owners allowed their slaves to keep part of the money they earned and to buy their freedom.

A South Carolina slave named Tom Molineaux won his freedom in an unusual way. He was a fine boxer, and his master would match him in fights against slaves on other plantations. Molineaux was promised his freedom if he won a fight on which his master had bet a lot of money. Tom won the fight and his freedom. He went to New York and continued boxing. Finally he worked his way to England where, as the American heavyweight champion, he lost two fights to the world champion, Tom Cribb.

In the cities of the South, slaves had a better life than on the plantations. Some men worked in factories or on the railroads. They worked in construction trades such as carpentry, bricklaying, and ironworking. In some southern cities there were more blacks than whites in these skilled jobs. In some ways, slaves in the cities had as much freedom as free blacks. They moved about pretty much as they pleased. Some even lived apart from their masters. But that still did not make them free.

Free Black Americans, South and North

Of course not all Black Americans were slaves. In 1850, perhaps one Black American in eight was free. In the South some free blacks worked as farmhands, and a few owned farms themselves. But most lived in the larger cities of the South where a skilled worker could make good money. Those without skills could find such work as ditch digging or street cleaning. Women worked as seamstresses. Both men and women were house servants. Others became shopkeepers, barbers, and restaurant owners. There were even a few doctors, architects, and dentists among the free blacks of the South.

But free blacks were feared by white southerners. They had to carry "free papers" which proved they weren't runaway slaves. If they lost these papers, they could be sold into slavery again. A free Black American in the South might be whipped, just like a slave. He or she might be

Black Americans: Reading Comprehension No. 2412

sold into slavery as punishment for a minor crime. Even so, many slaves who escaped the plantations and managed not to be caught were able to live as free men and women in the cities.

In the North, Black Americans knew that freedom was not the same as equality. Though there was no slavery, and free blacks had more rights than in the South, few whites looked upon blacks as equals. Blacks could vote in only a few states. As in the South, some Black Americans worked at skilled jobs, but most were ordinary laborers or house servants. White mobs rioted against free blacks in New York, Cincinnati, and other cities. In most places, they were kept out of "white" schools and places of entertainment.

But in the North, there was more opportunity for Black Americans to get an education than in the South. There were Black American writers, college professors, doctors, lawyers, artists, and scientists. Phyllis Wheatley, born in Africa, became one of America's best-known poets when she was only 17 years old. Later she was given her freedom. Benjamin Banneker was America's leading astronomer and helped plan the city of Washington, D.C. Ira Aldridge was one of America's greatest actors. When racism made it hard for him to appear in plays in his own country, he went to Europe where he became famous. Robert Morris was a lawyer who led the fight against "white only" schools in Massachusetts.

Tom Molineaux

Phyllis Wheatley

Benjamin Banneker

Ira Aldridge

Questions and Activities for Chapter 2

Name _____ Date _____

I. UNDERSTANDING THE WORDS

indentured	independence	economy	discipline
permanent	taunting	branding	domestic
indigo	incident	concerning	architects
mobs	prosperous	majority	equality
regulating	privileges	overseer	

A. *Find the four adjectives in the box above. Write the adjectives that mean:*

   1. rich _____

   2. for all time _____

   3. working at household jobs _____

   4. bound by a contract _____

B. *Find four verbs in the box ending in* **ing.** *Write the verbs that mean:*

   5. making rules for _____

   6. having to do with _____

   7. teasing _____

   8. burning a mark into the skin _____

C. *The remaining words in the box are all nouns. Write the words that mean:*

   9. freedom _____

   10. control gained through threat of punishment _____

   11. a happening _____

   12. building designers _____

   13. disorderly groups of people _____

   14. more than half the people _____

   15. a blue dye made from plants _____

   16. advantages _____

   17. supervisor of slaves on a plantation _____

   18. a condition of being the same for every person _____

   19. a system of production, buying, and selling _____

II. UNDERSTANDING THE FACTS

Circle the letter of the word or phrase that best completes each sentence.

  1. The first 20 Black Americans
        a) were slaves in Virginia.   b) were born in Holland.
           c) were indentured servants, not slaves.

  2. By 1700, there were black slaves
        a) in all of England's American colonies.
      b) only in the South.   c) only in Virginia.

  3. A plantation is a
        a) factory.   b) large farm.   c) ship.

4. One reason slavery took hold more strongly in the South than in the North was that
   a) more labor was needed for farming in the South.
   b) black people didn't live in the North.   c) northerners hated slavery.

5. The chapter implies that most slaves worked
   a) 8-10 hours a day.   b) 10-12 hours a day.   c) more than 12 hours a day.

6. _____ was a hero of the Battle of Bunker Hill.
   a) Crispus Attucks   b) Salem Poor   c) Mark Starlin

7. An invention that changed the way white southerners looked at slavery was the
   a) cotton gin.   b) automobile.   c) tractor.

8. Most southern plantations had
   a) over 200 slaves.   b) 50-100 slaves.   c) fewer than 20 slaves.

9. Most white southerners in 1850
   a) did not own slaves and thought slavery was wrong.
   b) owned slaves.   c) did not own slaves but saw nothing wrong with slavery.

10. Most plantation slaves worked as
   a) house servants.   b) field hands.   c) hunters.

11. _____ usually fared better than most other slaves.
   a) Field hands on plantations
   b) Skilled workers on plantations   c) Slaves who lived in cities

12. Free blacks in the South
   a) had to carry papers proving that they were free.
   b) could be whipped like a slave.   c) both a and b.

13. Most free blacks in the North
   a) could not vote.   b) were not allowed to learn to read or write.   c) were skilled workers.

14. Benjamin Banneker was a famous
   a) poet.   b) lawyer.   c) astronomer.

15. Ira Aldridge was a famous
   a) boxer.   b) actor.   c) poet.

III. THOUGHTS OF YOUR OWN

Use a separate sheet of paper to answer these questions.

1. List seven restrictions against slaves (things that slaves weren't allowed to do) that were included in the slave codes. Which of these do you think you would find particularly hard to live with? Why?

2. How do you think people could feel that it was right to hold other people as property?

3. Older history books have called Crispus Attucks a hero of the American struggle for independence. Recent ones don't seem to make too much of what he did. What do you think? (Give reasons.) Why do you think people's ideas about Attucks have changed? What makes a person a "hero?"

4. Why do you think white southerners' attitudes toward slavery changed from seeing it as a "necessary evil" to seeing it as a "positive good?"

5. Write a short dialogue (like a play) among the following people: a plantation field hand, a cook at the plantation house, a free black seamstress in a southern city, and a free black carpenter in a northern city. They should talk about their ways of life, their feelings, and their hopes for the future.

IV. FOR FAST WORKERS

Write a one- or two-page report about one of the Black Americans mentioned in this chapter or on one of those listed below. Use your school or public library to find the information.

   Peter Salem, *soldier*   Richard Allen, *minister*   Frances Harper, *poet*
   Edmonia Lewis, *sculptor*   James P. Beckworth, *explorer and frontiersman*

Chapter 3

THE FIGHT AGAINST SLAVERY

The first fighters against slavery were the slaves themselves. From the earliest days, masters complained of their "property" running away. Slaves would run away to freedom whenever they could. They would escape to the free states of the North and to Canada. They would run off to the frontier and live among the Indians.

But the penalties for trying to run away were harsh. Whipping was the least of it. Torture and mutilation were common. A slave from one of the states of the upper South who tried to run away was likely be "sold down the river" (the Mississippi) to a cotton plantation in the deep South. Here a slave's life was even harder and the chance for escape was practically zero.

Slaves resisted slavery in other ways. One way was by not taking the trouble to work hard; by appearing to be slow and stupid; and by deliberately damaging tools and machinery. But slave owners, whether or not they were fooled by such actions, used them as an excuse for slavery. The poor persons of color, they said, needed the "protection" of their masters. Of course the accomplishments of free Black Americans proved over and over that this was a lie.

There were other, more violent ways of resisting slavery. Slaves would chop off their own hand or foot to make themselves useless for work. Many slaves committed suicide. There were also cases of slaves poisoning their masters' food, killing a hated master or overseer in the fields, setting fire to barns and houses, and other acts of violence. Of course the violence done by slaves against their masters was practically nothing compared with the violence the slaves suffered at the hands of their masters.

Slave Rebellions

Because of the masters' control, organized slave revolts were few. But that didn't keep slave owners from worrying about them all the time. Nothing so frightened white southerners as the thought of a rebellion by their slaves. After all, in some parts of the South black people outnumbered whites by two to one. The news of the great revolt in Haiti in the 1790s, in which slaves and free blacks combined to throw out their hated French masters, was particularly frightening to American slave owners. What if "their own" blacks were to try the same thing?

Sometimes they did try it. Slave rebellions began when slavery did, and did not end until slavery ended. Most of them involved only a few slaves and were quickly put down. But slaves kept on preferring to die resisting than to continue to live as slaves. In Virginia in 1800, a group of about 600 slaves led by Gabriel Prosser collected weapons and planned to march on Richmond, the state capital. But a violent rainstorm delayed their attack, and two slaves informed the whites. Many slaves were arrested and 35 were executed. In 1811, more than 400 slaves in Louisiana rose in rebellion. It took the United States Army to stop them. In 1822, a free black carpenter in South Carolina named Denmark Vesey organized a revolt. It involved many free black people as well as slaves, and even a few whites as well. But the plot was discovered. Vesey and 135 others were hanged.

The capture of Nat Turner.

The revolt that most frightened the South was the one led by Nat Turner in Virginia. He was a deeply mystical person who believed that he had been chosen by God to deliver his people from slavery. In Feburary, 1831, there was a total eclipse of the sun. Turner took this as a sign to him to lead his people in revolt. He collected a small group of followers and set the Fourth of July as the date. When he became ill, Turner put off the revolt until he saw another sign. On August 13, when the sun turned a "peculiar greenish blue," he thought it was time.

The revolt began on August 21 with the killing of Turner's own master, Joseph Travis, and his family. Other families soon fell before the blows of the slaves. Within 24 hours, 60 whites had been killed and the revolt was spreading rapidly. Then the main group of rebels was met and overpowered by soldiers. More than 100 slaves were killed, and 13 slaves and two free blacks were immediately hanged. Turner was captured on October 30 and was hanged 12 days later.

Turner's rebellion terrified the South. Legislatures in many states called emergency sessions. They passed laws restricting even further the rights of slaves and free blacks. Many white southerners honestly could not understand why slaves would want to rebel against their kindly rule. They blamed Turner's revolt on the *abolitionists,* a group of white people and free blacks in the North.

The Abolitionists

People had been speaking out against slavery in America as early as the 1600s. The religious group known as the Quakers had been especially active in fighting slavery. Even some slave owners like Thomas Jefferson had seen slavery as an evil that would tear the country apart some day (though he himself freed his slaves only when he died). Many people were opposed to slavery but couldn't agree with forcing the slave owners to give up their slaves. They thought that slavery would die out by itself.

But in the 1820s, there appeared a new group of militant fighters against slavery. They wanted to put an immediate end to slavery—to *abolish* it.

Perhaps the first of the great abolitionists was David Walker. He had been born free in North Carolina but had moved to Massachusetts where he worked for *Freedom's Journal,* the first newspaper to be published by Black Americans. In 1829, he wrote the article that became known as

William Lloyd Garrison   Lydia Child   Frederick Douglass

David Walker's Appeal, in which he called upon all slaves to rise in revolt against their masters.

Other abolitionists did not favor violence, but they did demand an end to slavery at once. They fought slavery by writing books and articles and by making speeches that awakened people to the evil. They sent letters and petitions to Congress, and helped to support schools and colleges that educated former slaves. One of their leaders was William Lloyd Garrison, a white newspaper editor. In his newspaper, *The Liberator,* Garrison set down his challenge to slavery when he wrote: "I will be as harsh as truth and as uncompromising as justice. On this subject, I do not wish to think, to speak, or write with moderation. . . . I am in earnest . . . I will not excuse—I will not retreat a single inch—AND I WILL BE HEARD."

Arthur Tappan and his brother Lewis were rich New York businessmen who gave huge amounts of money to the fight against slavery. One person they helped was Prudence Crandall, who ran a school in Connecticut. When she admitted a black girl to her school, white parents took their children out. Later, when she opened a school for black children, people in the town wrecked her school and had her arrested.

Elijah Lovejoy was attacked and his printing press wrecked five times by mobs for publishing abolitionist newspapers in Missouri and Illinois. The sixth time, Lovejoy was killed.

Lydia Child, a famous writer of children's books, started her own anti-slavery newspaper. Southern bookstores stopped carrying her children's books.

Angelina and Sarah Grimké, sisters whose father was a slave-owning judge in South Carolina, moved to the North and became abolitionist speakers.

Former slaves were often the most effective abolitionist speakers. Here were people who could tell of the horrors of slavery first-hand and whose backs bore the scars of whips. Among the best-known black abolitionists were William Wells Brown, Samuel Cornish, and Henry Highland Garret. A former slave named Isabella, better known as Sojourner Truth, traveled through the North making moving speeches in which she expressed her fierce hatred of slavery.

The greatest of all the abolitionists was Frederick Douglass. He was born a slave in Maryland where his master's wife taught him to read and write. As a teenager, he escaped to the North. In 1841 he became active in the abolitionist movement. He was a handsome, powerful man with a deep, resonant voice, and was much sought after as a speaker. His newspaper, *The North Star,* became one of the leading abolitionist newspapers. Douglass often shared speakers' platforms with William Lloyd Garrison and other white abolitionists. But unlike them, he saw nothing wrong with slaves using violence to free themselves. Douglass remained a prominent Black American leader until his death in 1895. Toward the end of his life, he became the first Black American to be appointed ambassador to a foreign country (Haiti).

The Underground Railroad

The abolitionists did more than just make

A group of slaves escaping along the Underground Railroad.

speeches and write articles. They also helped more than 100,000 slaves escape to freedom.

In 1831, a slave named Tice Davids escaped from his master in Kentucky and crossed the Ohio River. Though his master was following him closely, he lost all trace of him on the northern side of the river. He said that his slave must have "gone off on the Underground Railroad."

The Underground Railroad became the name for the network of people who helped slaves to escape. There were laws against this, and people who were caught were sent to prison. But the people who helped runaways felt that they were obeying a "higher law."

All routes on the Underground Railroad started in slave country and headed north. They were dangerous routes, up rivers and over mountains. Masters, sheriffs, and professional slave catchers would come after the runaways. Movement was almost always at night, when it was safer. Slaves used the North Star to guide them. On cloudy nights, when there were no stars, they would feel for moss on the tree trunks. (It always grows on the north side of trees.)

Because moving at night was slow, the "stations" were usually only 10 to 20 miles apart. By day, the runaways were hidden in the barns and homes of abolitionists who were the "conductors" on the railroad. Here the slaves rested, ate, and waited for the next night's trip. Word would be passed to the next "station" that runaways were on the way.

Sometimes the "conductors" gave rides to their passengers. They carried them in wagons and carriages built with secret compartments. One escaping slave, Henry "Box" Brown, was shipped from Virginia to Pennsylvania in a packing case!

More than 3,200 men and women helped out along the Underground Railroad. Levi Coffin, a Quaker who lived in Indiana, was called the "president" of the railroad. He helped more than 3,000 escaping slaves along their way. John Fairfield was the son of a rich Virginia slave-owner, but he hated slavery himself. He helped a friend who was a slave escape to the North, then returned south many times to lead other slaves out. He was a master of disguises and of daring plans. Once he led out 28 slaves at once by disguising them as a funeral procession.

The best-known conductor on the Underground Railroad was Harriet Tubman, who was an escaped slave herself. She made 19 trips back to the South and freed more than 300 people, including her parents, her sister, and her two children. She carried a gun and threatened to shoot any runaway who wanted to turn back. Usually she would start her escapes on Saturday night. This gave her a head start because news of runaways wasn't posted until Monday morning. Later, during the Civil War, she was a spy for the Union Army. There was a reward of $50,000 for her capture. Conductor Harriet Tubman never lost a passenger and earned herself the nickname, "Moses."

Harriet Tubman

War Grows Nearer

The abolitionists and the Underground Railroad helped to deepen the growing split between North and South. It seemed clear that America was moving close to a war between the two sections, a war in which slavery would be one of the main concerns. In 1850, Congress passed a tough *fugitive slave law* as part of an agreement meant to hold the nation together. Now southern slave hunters could come into northern states in search of runaways. More and more northerners refused to obey the laws against helping runaways, and Underground Railroad conductors began taking their passengers all the way to Canada. In the ten years between 1850 and 1860, one event after another helped to drive North and South further apart.

Black soldiers of the Union Army.

One of these events was the publication of a book. In 1852, an abolitionist writer named Harriet Beecher Stowe published a novel called *Uncle Tom's Cabin.* It was a story of slaves on plantations in the South and of the cruelties of the slave system. The book sold 300,000 copies in less than a year, and Stowe became the most famous author in the United States. Northern readers accepted the book as fact. Many more northerners became enemies of slavery. Southerners charged that *Uncle Tom's Cabin* was full of lies and pointed out that Stowe had never even visited the South. The book was banned in most southern cities. Probably no other book in our history has affected national events as much as *Uncle Tom's Cabin*. When Harriet Beecher Stowe met President Abraham Lincoln in 1862, he said, "So this is the little lady who caused the big war."

Black Americans in the Civil War

The "big war" broke out soon after the election of President Lincoln in 1860. Lincoln was not an abolitionist, but he was opposed to allowing slavery to spread to any new states. To the South, this was just one step away from outlawing slavery altogether. Eleven southern states left the Union and set up a separate country, the Confederate States of America, (referred to as the Confederacy). In April, 1861, the war between the North and South began.

At first, the Civil War was not a war to free the slaves but to keep the Union together. "If I could save the Union without freeing any slave I would do it. If I could save the Union by freeing all the slaves, I would do it," Lincoln said in 1862. Black Americans, however, saw the war as their chance for freedom. In the North, hundreds of thousands of blacks volunteered to fight for the Union Army. At first, they were turned down because of the country's old policy of not allowing blacks to serve in the army. But when the war did not end quickly, as many had expected it would, this policy was changed.

Nearly 200,000 black men served in the Union Army, some as officers. Nearly 70,000 were killed. If a black soldier was captured, he was treated not as a prisoner of war, but as a runaway slave.

Black civilians also contributed to the war effort. Women worked in hospitals and army camps. Others formed groups to raise money and to distribute food and clothing to the soldiers. In some parts of the North, blacks were blamed by some whites as being the cause of the war. When poor whites in New York City rioted in 1863 to protest being drafted into the Union Army, they invaded the black sections of town, beating and killing free blacks and burning their houses.

On January 1, 1863, President Lincoln issued the *Emancipation Proclamation*, freeing all the slaves in territories still in rebellion against the Union. Of course, there was no power to enforce this proclamation where the Confederacy was still in power. But whenever the Union Army came near, slaves would free themselves by running away and finding the soldiers, or simply by refusing to work. By the time the war ended, on April 9, 1865, it was clear that slavery was no longer going to exist in the United States. But just how the lives of Black Americans would be changed by emancipation, no one was yet able to say.

Abraham Lincoln

Questions and Activities for Chapter 3

Name _____ Date _____

I. UNDERSTANDING THE WORDS

frontier	rebellion	uncompromising	civilians
mutilation	legislatures	resonant	emancipation
deliberately	sessions	barred	proclamation
accomplishments	militant	policy	executed
petitions			

Complete the crossword puzzle using words from the box.

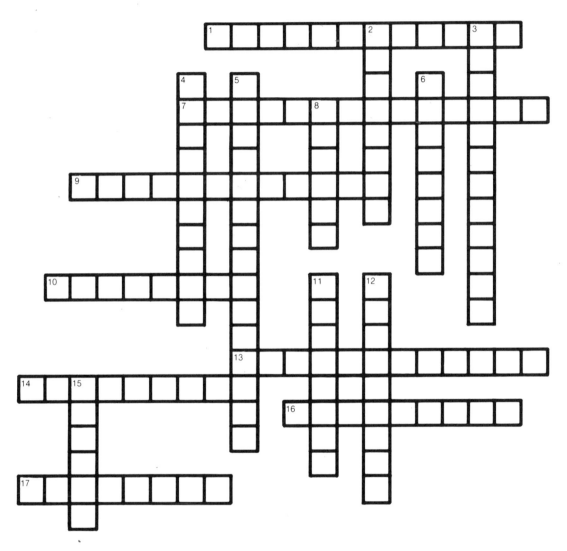

Across Clues
1. on purpose
7. standing firm
9. announcement
10. meetings
13. setting free
14. revolt
16. not soldiers
17. killed by law

Down Clues
2. sounding deep and rich
3. law-making groups
4. cutting off part of the body
5. deeds done
6. having a fighting spirit
8. plan for a course of action
11. edge of settled country
12. letters demanding a certain action
15. forbidden, kept out

II. UNDERSTANDING THE FACTS

Answer the questions and fill in the blanks.

1. List at least four ways that slaves resisted their masters.

_____

_____

_____

_____

2. Name three people who led slave rebellions. _____

_____

3. _____ was the abolitionist who published *The Liberator*.

4. _____ was an abolitionist who was a famous writer of children's books.

5. _____ was the abolitionist who opened a school for black children.

6. _____ was the abolitionist who published *The North Star*.

7. A slave named Isabella who became a leading abolitionist speaker went by the name

_____ .

8. _____ was the abolitionist who was killed by a mob in Illinois.

9. Who was known as the "president" of the Underground Railroad? _____

10. Who was the leading "conductor" on the Railroad? _____

   What was her nickname? _____

11. In 1850, Congress passed a tough fugitive slave law. *Fugitive* means _____

_____ .

12. Harriet Beecher Stowe's famous novel about slavery was called _____ .

III. THOUGHTS OF YOUR OWN

Use a separate sheet of paper to answer these questions.

1. "Slaves should not be criticized for anything they did to free themselves from slavery." Do you agree? Why or why not?
2. The abolitionists wrote letters to the government, gave speeches, published newspapers, and gave money to fight slavery. Do you think this helped the fight against slavery very much? Give reasons for your answer.
3. Write a story or a short play about a family of slaves escaping on the Underground Railroad.

IV. FOR FAST WORKERS

Write a one- or two-page report about one of the Black Americans mentioned in this chapter or one of those listed below. Use your school or public library to find the information.

Robert Smalls, *war hero and congressman*   Martin R. Delany, *abolitionist*

Chapter 4

EMANCIPATED, BUT NOT FREE

In the last months of the war and afterward, people in the South suffered terribly. Money was worthless, land was abandoned, food had been destroyed, cities had been burned. There was no law except "might makes right."

Millions of blacks who had worked only for their masters now had to decide what to do to avoid starvation. "They turned us loose like a bunch of stray dogs," one ex-slave remembered years later. "No homes, no clothing, no nothing. . . . All we had to farm with were sharp sticks. We'd stick holes and plant corn."

The government in Washington set up the *Freedmen's Bureau* to help the ex-slaves. The Bureau furnished supplies and medical care, found jobs for ex-slaves, and leased and sold abandoned land to blacks. It built 46 hospitals, over 4,000 schools, and many churches.

The Bureau's plan was to give land—"40 acres and a mule"—to any black family who wanted it. By 1870, 30,000 ex-slaves had been settled on abandoned land. But the government didn't think it was right to take land away from its owners (except for those who had been important Confederate officials). There wasn't enough land to go around. Many freed slaves ended up on the plantations again, working for their old masters. They were allowed to farm a piece of land in exchange for rent in the form of a share of the crops they raised. These farmers became known as *sharecroppers*. Many poor white farmers became sharecroppers too.

Some of the freed slaves went north. Many more drifted west into the newly opened territories. During the days of the "wild west," as many as a third of the cowboys and U.S. Cavalry soldiers were black.

Reconstruction

Meanwhile, back in Washington, D.C., the government had to decide how to deal with the defeated South. Abraham Lincoln had never meant to give Black Americans full equality with whites. "The Emancipation Proclamation," one abolitionist complained, "frees the slave but ignores the Negro." Had Lincoln lived, many people believe that he would have come to favor complete equality for blacks and whites. But on April 14, 1865, Lincoln was assassinated.

The new President, Andrew Johnson, meant to carry out Lincoln's plan of giving back to the white southerners their land and power. The old slave codes in most of the southern states were replaced by "black codes." They gave blacks the right to own property and to make contracts, but little else. In most ways, the black codes were not much different from the slave codes.

A storm of protest came from the North. A group of congressmen called the *radicals* were determined to create their own program of *reconstruction* for the South. Reconstruction, as they saw it, would mean complete equality for blacks. The southern states would not be readmitted to the union until white voters accepted black equality. Until then, U.S. troops would be stationed in the South to enforce the new laws.

Led by the radicals, Congress passed three new amendments to the Constitution. The 13th Amendment ended slavery in the United States forever. The 14th Amendment made all Americans equal citizens and gave them equal protection of the laws. The 15th Amendment gave all male citizens the right to vote. (Women did not win the right to vote until 1919.) Strict new *civil rights* laws were passed to enforce the new amendments.

Under Reconstruction, white southerners were not allowed to vote until they had taken an oath of loyalty to the United States. Until then, southern state governments were run largely by northerners and southern blacks. During reconstruction, 16 blacks were elected to Congress and two, Blanche K. Bruce and Hiram Revels, to the U.S. Senate. Dozens were elected to state legislatures.

White southerners were outraged that so many of the new voters and lawmakers were ex-slaves, some of whom could barely read and write. But as Frederick Douglass said, "If the Negro knows enough to pay taxes, he knows enough to vote; if he knows enough to fight for the flag . . . he knows enough to vote." But whites had spent too many years seeing blacks as slaves and inferiors to accept them as equals that easily. One congressman spoke frankly of the problem of racism when he said, "The real trouble is that *we hate the Negro.* It is not his ignorance that offends us, but his color."

Some white southerners formed secret clubs to keep blacks "in their place" through violence and terror. The biggest of these groups was the Ku Klux Klan. It began in Tennessee and soon spread throughout the South. Its purpose was to keep blacks from voting or from exercising their other newly won rights. In some cases, fright was enough to persuade them. Black people learned to dread the strange costumes of the Klansmen—black robes with red crosses on the breast and white circles around the eyes of the hood. The Klan would use threats or sometimes burn a cross in front of someone's home. If that didn't work, they would burn down the house. Blacks who resisted the Klan were whipped, tarred and feathered, or lynched—killed by hanging, shooting, or burning alive. White northerners working in the Reconstruction governments (the so-called "scalawags") met the same fate. The Klan murdered successful freedmen, burned black schools, and shot men who tried to help blacks register to vote. After 1876, the Klan began to die off, but it was revived again in the early 1900s. This time it terrorized not only blacks but also Jews, Catholics, and foreign-born Americans. The Ku Klux Klan still exists

Ex-slaves, now free, voting for the first time.
(from an old photograph)

The Ku Klux Klan spread terror among the freed slaves.

today. It is not the serious problem it once was, but it still does a great deal of mischief and harm.

Reconstruction ended in 1876. Many of the radicals who had supported it in Congress were dead or had been voted out of office. Courts had largely stopped enforcing the laws that had been passed to secure equality for blacks. Finally, as the result of a "deal" among politicians, the federal troops were pulled out of the South. Black Americans were on their own.

Jim Crow

"Jim Crow" was the name of a popular song and dance that an actor named Thomas Rice said he had seen done by an old black man in Kentucky. But in the South, "Jim Crow" came to mean a system of laws. The Jim Crow laws legalized *segregation,* or forced separation, of blacks from whites. They made Black Americans second-class citizens by law.

Segregation laws were passed in states across the South from 1880 to about 1910. There had long been segregation in the North, too, but the Jim Crow laws made it formal and specific. Blacks were forced to ride on separate railroad cars and streetcars. There were separate Jim Crow sections on boats. There were Jim Crow restaurants, schools, hotels, hospitals, parks, ball fields, restrooms, telephone booths, and drinking fountains, each with its sign reading "white only" or "colored only." In most stores, blacks had to use separate rear entrances and wait until all white customers had been served. There were separate "colored entrances" to theaters; blacks had to sit in the balcony.

Southern states passed laws requiring a *literacy test* or *poll tax* before a person could vote. A literacy test required a voter to be able to read. If a black person mispronounced one word, he flunked the test. Sometimes a white person would be given the town newspaper to read for his test, while a black person would be given a difficult book or a newspaper in a foreign language. The literacy test and poll taxes often kept poor whites from voting, too, but some southern states had a way around that. It was called the *grandfather clause*. A man did not have to pay the poll tax or take the literacy test if his grandfather had been a voter. Of course, this excluded the former slaves.

All these laws were upheld by the courts. The U.S. Supreme Court ruled that if a state law *looked* as if it was being applied fairly to all people, the court would not hear any cases challenging the law. In 1892, the Supreme Court ruled in the case of *Plessy vs. Ferguson.* Plessy was a black man who had been forced to ride on a segregated railroad car in Louisiana. The court ruled that there was nothing wrong with segregation as long as the railroad cars for blacks and whites were equal in comfort and service. "Separate but equal" became the test that made Jim Crow legal for the next 62 years. Of course, separate was rarely equal. The accommodations for blacks in railroad cars, restaurants, and other places were nearly always older, shabbier, and less-well serviced. In 1912, the average amount of tax money spent for each child in the public schools of the United States was $15. For black children in segregated schools, it was $1.71. Separate was clearly not equal—but it was the law just the same.

Lynching, of course, was against the law. But it was often used by lawless whites to keep Black Americans "in their place." Lynching means the killing of a person by a mob. From 1884 to 1916, there were more than 3,600 lynchings in the United States. All but a few took place in the South, and in more than eight out of ten cases, the victim was black. In 1901 alone, 130 Ameri-cans were lynched. The victims were accused of crimes ranging from murder to "insulting a white person." Lynching usually meant death by hanging, but some victims were burned alive or tortured in other ways.

A black newspaperwoman, Ida B. Wells, was one of the few people to speak out publicly against lynching. She started her own news-paper, *Free Speech*, in Memphis, Tennessee when she was only 22 years old. After a mob wrecked her printing press, she carried on her work in the North. She pressed for a federal anti-lynching law. Such a law was proposed to Congress in 1900, and similar laws continued to be proposed well into the 1940s. No such law was ever passed.

Jim Crow signs like these were common all over the South until the 1970s.

Questions and Activities for Chapter 4

Name _____ Date _____

I. UNDERSTANDING THE WORDS

A. *Circle the letter of the answer that means the same as the underlined word in each sentence. Use a dictionary if you need help.*

1. After the Civil War, much land in the South was <u>abandoned.</u>
   a) useless for farming   b) destroyed by gunfire   c) given up; empty

2. People did what they could to avoid <u>starvation.</u>
   a) being killed by roving gangs   b) dying from hunger   c) going to jail

3. President Lincoln was <u>assassinated.</u>
   a) voted out of power   b) murdered   c) sent to jail for a crime

4. Congress passed three new <u>amendments</u> to the Constitution.
   a) pages   b) changes   c) rules

5. Civil rights laws were passed to <u>enforce</u> the new amendments.
   a) explain   b) make sure they're observed   c) change

6. The Ku Klux Klan was <u>revived</u> in the early 1900s.
   a) started up again   b) outlawed   c) made safe

7. Reconstruction ended as the result of a deal among <u>politicians.</u>
   a) southern voters   b) people in the business of government   c) crooks

8. Black people were <u>excluded</u> from voting.
   a) made unwelcome   b) kept separate   c) kept out

9. The <u>accommodations</u> for blacks under the Jim Crow laws were nearly always poorer and shabbier.
   a) laws   b) restaurants   c) things or places that fill a need

10. By 1876, the courts had largely stopped enforcing laws that had been passed to <u>secure</u> equality for blacks.
    a) disavow   b) obtain   c) disassemble

11. Blacks who <u>resisted</u> the Klan were whipped, tarred and feathered, or lynched.
    a) supported   b) joined   c) opposed

12. In the late 1800s many Jim Crow laws were <u>upheld</u> by the courts.
    a) struck down   b) supported   c) initiated

13. The southern states would not be <u>readmitted</u> to the Union until white voters accepted black equality.
    a) allowed to return   b) traded   c) segregated

B. *Be a word detective!* The word *lynch* was originally a person's name. Look in a dictionary or encyclopedia to find out who he was and how his name came to mean *murder by mob*. Use a separate sheet of paper to write a paragraph explaining it.

II. UNDERSTANDING THE FACTS

Match each term with the word or phrase below that best describes it. Write the correct letter next to the number.

_____ 1. Freedmen's Bureau

_____ 2. Confederate

_____ 3. sharecroppers

_____ 4. Reconstruction

_____ 5. radicals

_____ 6. 13th Amendment

_____ 7. 14th Amendment

_____ 8. 15th Amendment

_____ 9. Ku Klux Klan

_____ 10. carpetbaggers

_____ 11. scalawags

_____ 12. segregation

_____ 13. Jim Crow

_____ 14. poll tax and literacy test

A. a secret club that terrorized black people

B. referring to the South during the Civil War

C. ended slavery in the United States

D. the northerners' plan for rebuilding the South after the war

E. forced separation (of groups of people)

F. a nickname for the system of segregation in the South

G. gave all citizens equal protection of the laws

H. northerners working in southern state governments after the Civil War

I. an organization that helped the freed slaves

J. a group of congressmen who tried to bring about change in the South

K. farmers working on land owned by others and paying part of what they grew as rent

L. two kinds of laws passed to keep black people from voting

M. white southerners who helped the Reconstruction governments

N. gave black men the right to vote

III. THOUGHTS OF YOUR OWN

Use a separate sheet of paper to answer these questions.

1. What is meant by the phrase "might makes right?" Do you agree with the idea? Why or why not?

2. "The Emancipation Proclamation frees the slave but ignores the Negro." What do you think this statement means?

3. Take the point of view of a white southerner in the years after Reconstruction. How do you feel about what's going on? What do you think is a fair way to deal with the newly freed slaves?

4. Why didn't "separate but equal" work out that way? Do you think people could ever be equal under a system like "Jim Crow?" Give reasons for your answer.

IV. FOR FAST WORKERS

Write a one- or two-page report about one of the Black Americans mentioned in this chapter or one of those listed below. Use your school or public library to find the information.

P.B.S. Pinchback, *politician*

John H. Rock, *lawyer*

Granville T. Woods, *inventor*

Paul Lawrence Dunbar, *poet*

Henry O. Tanner, *artist*

Charles W. Chestnutt, *writer*

Chapter 5

LOOKING for SOLUTIONS

During the bleak years after Reconstruction, Black Americans had little to be hopeful about. The promise of freedom had proven to be an empty one. Black communities were held together largely by close family life and by churches. For years the black churches had been more than just places for religious worship. They were social centers and community meeting places for education and protest.

Education became a passion for many Black Americans after slavery ended. As one former slave described it, "It was a whole race trying to go to school. Few were too young, and none too old, to make the attempt to learn. As fast as any teachers could be secured, not only were day schools filled, but night schools as well. The great ambition of the older people was to try to learn to read the Bible before they died. . . . Men and women who were 50 and 75 years old would be found in the night schools. Sunday schools were formed shortly after freedom, but the principal book studied in Sunday school was the spelling book. Day school, night school, and Sunday school were always crowded, and often many had to be turned away for want of room."

The Age of Booker T. Washington

The former slave who wrote those words was the best-known Black American of his day. Booker T. Washington was 16 years old in 1872 when he entered the Hampton Institute in Virginia. This was a school for blacks that had been founded by a northern Civil War general. At Hampton, students were taught *vocational* education—useful trades and skills. Young men learned carpentry and bricklaying; young women learned sewing and homemaking skills. Booker T. Washington saw vocational education as the hope for Black Americans. He believed that labor not only helped one make money, but also built a person's character and intelligence.

In 1881, Washington and a few students founded Tuskegee Institute in Alabama. It became the country's leading school for the vocational education of Black Americans. By 1900, Washington was being hailed as the leader of his people. Very few matters concerning race relations came up without Washington being called upon to give his advice. In 1905, he became the first Black American to have dinner at the White House, as a guest of President Theodore Roosevelt.

One reason whites were so eager to hail Washington as a black leader was that he didn't seek equality for blacks. He stressed respect for the law and cooperation with white authorities. In his most famous speech, given in Atlanta in 1895, he said, "To those of my race . . . who underestimate the importance of cultivating friendly relations with the southern white men . . . I would say cast down your bucket where you are—cast it down in making friends . . . with the people of all races."

One Black American leader called this speech Washington's "Atlanta compromise." This was William Edward Burghart Du Bois. W.E.B. Du Bois was born in Massachusetts and had never been a slave. He had very different ideas about the education of blacks and their relations with whites. In the North there were colleges and universities that had been started by abolitionists and had always accepted black students. In the South there were colleges and universities for blacks that had been started after the Civil War by rich northern whites. Du Bois himself had graduated from one of these schools, Fisk University, and had gone on to earn a doctorate from Harvard University. He placed his hope for the future on a "talented tenth" of young Black Americans who would receive a *broad* education.

If education were left to men like Washington, Du Bois thought, "Negro" colleges would turn out laborers and wage earners, but not people who could compete equally with whites. Besides, he felt that Washington's idea of vocational education was old-fashioned. Industry in America was changing. The old-style trades were becoming less useful. More and more laboring jobs were with big companies which would not hire blacks, no matter how skilled they were. Workers were forming labor unions, and most of these would not accept black members. Du Bois demanded for blacks the right to vote and the right to education according to ability. He was not as influential a leader as Washington, but his book, *The Souls of Black Folk,* became like a second Bible to many Black Americans when it was published in 1903. He would write many more books in his 95-year lifetime.

Organizing for Change

In 1905, Du Bois called a group of young, educated black men to a meeting at Niagara Falls, Canada. Calling themselves the Niagara Movement, they drew up a program for winning justice for Black Americans. They demanded freedom of speech, equal voting rights, an end to discrimination based on race (such as the Jim Crow laws), and the recognition of basic human rights (such as the right not to be lynched).

During those first years of the 20th century, the country experienced a number of riots

Booker T. Washington

W.E.B. De Bois

Black Americans: Reading Comprehension   No. 2412

The office of the NAACP's magazine, Crisis. *Dr. Du Bois is at the right.*
(from an old photograph)

directed against blacks. White mobs would invade the section of a city where blacks lived, beating, burning, and killing. Blacks would fight back, but the law would usually side with the white rioters. Sometimes these riots happened in northern cities. A particularly ugly one took place in Springfield, Illinois in 1908. Black men were lynched within two miles of Abraham Lincoln's grave.

Some of the young people of the Niagara Movement, together with some whites who were horrified by the riots, met in 1909 to form the National Association for the Advancement of Colored People (NAACP). This organization dedicated itself to using the court system to fight for an end to forced segregation, for equal education for black and white children, and for voting rights for blacks. Dr. Du Bois became the editor of the NAACP's magazine, *Crisis.*

The NAACP did win some victories. But the problem of racism was so huge that winning a few court cases could do little to change the lives of most Black Americans. Of special importance to the NAACP were the problems faced by blacks who were now moving by the tens of thousands from the South into the big cities of the North.

The Great Migration

Poverty was the main reason so many southerners, white and black, migrated to the North. In rural areas of the South, it had become almost impossible for many people to earn a living. There were jobs to be had in northern cities. Blacks were escaping from racism and terror as well as from poverty. In some parts of the South, black sharecropper farmers had been forced into a system called *peonage.* They found that they owed the landowner more money for the use of tools, clothes, and equipment than they could earn from selling the crops they raised. Often these amounts "owed" were false, but as one farmer later recalled, "not one of us would have dared to dispute the word of a white man." Sharecroppers became bound to the land until they could work off the debt—which was never. They were chained up to keep from running off, just as in slavery days. But many did run off— this time not on an underground railroad but on real trains, bound for Chicago, New York, Detroit, Philadelphia, and other northern cities.

As it turned out, there were not nearly as many jobs as there were people to fill them. Black men were kept out of most jobs. Black women found jobs as domestics—household servants. Once in the city, blacks also found it difficult to find decent housing. In most northern cities, blacks had long been forced to live in segregated areas and could not move into "white" neighborhoods. With more and more black people arriving from the South, the black neighborhoods became urban *ghettos*. Blacks were crowded together and forced to live in small, unsanitary homes. There were few recreational facilities such as parks and swimming pools open to blacks, and little money or space to build them.

The few blacks who were lucky enough to get an education or to build a successful business did not live in such misery. But they did live in the ghetto with their poorer brothers and sisters. They could not find housing outside it. Dick Gregory, an entertainer and civil-rights leader who became prominent in the 1960s, noted with bitter humor the difference between racism in the South and in the North: "Down there, they don't care how close I get as long as I don't get too big. Up here, they don't care how big I get as long as I don't get too close."

Still, Black Americans flocked to the North. It seemed to offer more hope than the South. An organization called the National Urban League helped blacks to find jobs and housing and to deal with their problems in the cities. The black newspapers, too, helped people adjust to the cities and offered news of interest to the black community that was ignored by other papers. The leading black newspaper was the Chicago *Daily Defender,* begun in 1905 by Robert S. Abbott. Others included the Pittsburgh *Courier,* the Baltimore *Afro-American News* and New York's *Amsterdam News.*

America's participation in World War I in 1917-1918 also seemed to hold promise for Black Americans. This, after all, was the war to "make the world safe for democracy." More than 370,000 Black Americans served in the armed forces during the war. They believed, as had earlier generations of Black Americans, that by serving their country they would have the right to demand better treatment after the war was over.

But Jim Crow followed Black Americans to war. Army units and training camps in the United States were segregated. On the battlefields, thousands of Black Americans were assigned to units of the French army, our allies against the Germans. The U.S. government advised the French not to treat the black soldiers as equals because it would offend white American

A street in Harlem, the black ghetto of New York City, about 1915.
(from an old photograph)

Black Americans: Reading Comprehension   No. 2412

soldiers! The French, who were happy to have all the help they could get, paid little attention to this racist advice. After the war, some Black American soldiers remained in Europe where they thought they'd have a better chance at equality.

Back home, there was more tension between blacks and whites. The returning soldiers competed with each other for jobs. More blacks were moving into previously all-white neighborhoods. The year 1919 saw the most violent race riots in our history. There were more than 20 major riots in cities throughout the country. The worst violence happened in Chicago. It started when a black boy was stoned to death after his raft drifted onto a "whites only" beach. In the riot that followed, 38 people were killed and 536 injured.

Some Black Americans now felt that they could no longer expect any justice from the United States. They sought a return to "Mother Africa." Their leader was a man from Jamaica named Marcus Garvey.

Marcus Garvey

More than any other black leader of his day, Garvey had a talent for reaching people. He was a showman who often staged street parades with brass bands and large feathered hats. In the mid-1920s, he had more than a million followers. Garvey's simple message was that Negro people should be proud of being black; that the black people of Africa and America had a glorious history from which they should claim a deep sense of self-respect. The only hope of Americn Negroes, he said, was to return to Africa and build a country of their own. He called on Black Americans, especially those of darker color, to follow him to Africa.

There had been "back-to-Africa" movements before. In the 1820s, freed slaves from America had started a colony in Africa that became the nation of Liberia. But Liberia had been a plan by whites to get free blacks out of the country. Marcus Garvey's program was supported by a mass movement of Black Americans themselves.

Garvey tried to get land in Africa to start a colony, but he was not successful. In 1921, he announced the beginning of the Empire of Africa and declared himself its president. But few Black Americans actually returned to Africa. Garvey was arrested in 1925 for using the mail to dishonestly raise money for his steamship company. Two years later, he was deported to Jamaica.

For most Black Americans, Africa was no solution to the problem of racism. They were Americans—even though it looked as if white Americans didn't want them. Since the days of slavery, Black Americans had been developing their own culture and their own art. The first great flowering of that culture was now taking place in Harlem, the black ghetto of New York City.

Questions and Activities for Chapter 5

Name _____ Date _____

I. UNDERSTANDING THE WORDS

bleak	founded	discrimination	facilities
passion	authorities	migration	participation
ambition	compromise	unsanitary	allies
character	influential	recreational	previously

A. *In the blank space after each sentence, write a word from the box above that means the same as the underlined part of the sentence. Use a dictionary if you need help.*

1. When the house burned down, our family faced a <u>dreary</u> future. _____

2. The two countries were <u>partners</u> in the war against their enemy. _____

3. The <u>people in charge</u> would not let Maria keep a wolf cub as a pet. _____

4. Until the YMCA was built, there were few <u>places for play and entertainment</u> in the neighborhood. *(two words)* _____ _____

5. Arthur had to deal with <u>prejudice</u> against foreigners when he went looking for a job.

   _____

6. The dinner honored my father, who had <u>started</u> the club 20 years ago. _____

7. She had a great <u>desire to achieve</u> fame as a musician. _____

8. He had never been to school, but he had a <u>burning</u> need for learning. _____

9. <u>In the past,</u> he had been highly <u>sought after</u> for his views on fighting crime. *(two words)*

   _____ _____

10. Richard got a lot of credit for <u>taking part</u> in school activities. _____

11. When we first came to the city, we lived in an apartment that was <u>neither clean nor healthful.</u>

    _____

12. In the early days of America, there was a great <u>mass movement</u> to the West. _____

13. People who believe in astrology think that <u>the kind of person one is</u> is determined by the

    stars. _____

14. Louise quit her job because too often she was called upon to <u>go against what she believed.</u>

    _____

B. *Be a word detective!* The word *ghetto* was originally an Italian word that may have meant either *gate* or *iron foundry.* How did it come to mean *a part of a city where members of a minority group are forced to live?* There were several steps involved in this change in meaning. Use a dictionary and encyclopedia to trace these steps. Explain them on a separate sheet of paper.

II. UNDERSTANDING THE FACTS

Circle T *if the statement is true. Circle* F *if the statement is false.*

T F 1. Churches were an important part of Black American social life.

T F 2. After emancipation, most Black Americans were too concerned about survival to worry about education.

T F 3. Booker T. Washington felt that most blacks should go to college.

T F 4. Booker T. Washington was a founder of the Hampton Institute.

T F 5. *Vocational education* means training in useful skills.

T F 6. Booker T. Washington and W.E.B. Du Bois agreed that Black Americans should demand equality with whites.

T F 7. Booker T. Washington had more of a following during his lifetime than did Du Bois.

T F 8. W.E.B. Du Bois was a highly educated man.

T F 9. Around 1900, most big companies did not hire black workers.

T F 10. Booker T. Washington's book, *The Souls of Black Folk,* was widely read by Black Americans.

T F 11. W.E.B. Du Bois was one of the founders of the Niagara Movement.

T F 12. The NAACP thought that rioting was the best way to win equal rights for blacks.

T F 13. *Peonage* was a system of forced labor.

T F 14. Blacks moving to the cities of the North found it easy to get work.

T F 15. Blacks with money did not usually live in the ghetto.

T F 16. Robert S. Abbott's New York *Daily Defender* was a leading black newspaper.

T F 17. Black Americans in World War I were not troubled by racism.

T F 18. America's French allies in World War I treated the black soldiers as equals.

T F 19. Marcus Garvey called upon Black Americans to return to Africa.

T F 20. Garvey was able to get land to start a colony in Africa.

III. THOUGHTS OF YOUR OWN

Use a separate sheet of paper to answer these questions.

1. In the debate over education between Booker T. Washington and W.E.B. Du Bois, which man do you think was right? Give reasons for your answer.

2. In the time period of this chapter, Black Americans had few rights and no power. Why do you think there were so many lynchings and riots directed against them?

3. Do you think it was right for farm workers to run away from their debts as described on page 36? Give reasons for your answer.

4. Explain what you think Dick Gregory may have meant by his statement on page 37.

5. Why do you think Marcus Garvey's back-to-Africa movement did not succeed?

IV. FOR FAST WORKERS

Write a one- or two-page report about one of the Black Americans mentioned in this chapter or one of those listed below. Use your school or public library to find the information.

Jesse Owens, *athlete*   Daniel Hale Williams, *doctor*   Matthew Henson, *explorer*
Jack Johnson, *boxer*   Mary McLeod Bethune, *educator*   George Washington Carver, *scientist*
Charles Drew, *doctor*   Josephine Baker, *entertainer*   James "Cool Papa" Bell, *baseball player*

Chapter 6

AN EXPLOSION of WORDS and MUSIC

These three stylish young Harlem women of the 1920s show that all was not poverty and despair in the ghettos.

The 1920s was one of the most interesting decades of the century. It was the beginning of modern America—the America of the automobile, mass entertainment, and sports idols. It was the jazz age—the time when the world was beginning to take notice of an exciting form of music created by Black Americans. It was also the time of the Harlem Renaissance—a golden age for Black American writers.

Renaissance is a French word that means *rebirth*. What was reborn in Harlem in the 1920s was Black American culture and a feeling of pride in that culture. There had been great black writers in America going back to slavery days. Phyllis Wheatley had been a well-known poet in the 1700s; Paul Lawrence Dunbar in the 1800s; Charles Waddell Chestnutt had written great novels and short stories dealing with the black experience in America. But the group of writers that lived and worked in Harlem in the 1920s represented a new beginning—an understanding by Black Americans that they could produce a literature as worthy as that of any people in the world.

A Few Voices

The Harlem Renaissance might be said to have begun with Claude McKay, whose book of poems, *Harlem Shadows,* was published in 1922. McKay later published several novels, but he is better known for his poems. He used forms of poetry that might have been familiar to Shakespeare. But he used them to express horror about race riots, lynchings, and other experiences of Black Americans.

Other famous writers of the Harlem Renaissance were Rudolph Fisher, Countee Cullen, Jean Toomer, Zora Neale Hurston, and Arna Bontemps. Novelist Richard Wright and poet Gwendolyn Brooks are sometimes considered part of the Harlem Renaissance, although they came along later and lived and worked in Chicago, not New York. (You don't have to memorize the names, but we include them in case you want to

look into some of their books.)

Probably the greatest and certainly the most famous of the Harlem writers was Langston Hughes. He was born in Kansas, lived in Mexico as a child, and came to New York as a young man. He wrote in all kinds of forms—poetry, songs, novels, short stories, plays, biography, history, and essays. The theme of all his work was ordinary people—in particular, everyday black people in Harlem and their joys, pleasures, and sorrows. Though his books are read and respected around the world, it can also be said that he was a true folk artist who wrote for the people he was writing about. His most famous character is an ordinary Harlem black man named Jesse B. Semple—"Simple," by nickname. Simple's adventures, loves, and views on life are the subject of story after story. But in one sense, it can be said that Langston Hughes's greatest character was Harlem itself and the rich experiences that black people found there.

The Harlem Renaissance died quite suddenly in the 1930s. These were the years of the Great Depression, and nearly everyone, black and white, was worried about basic survival. People who are worried about their next meal have much less time for art and culture. This doesn't mean that the writers stopped writing. It just means that few people could afford to buy their work.

Black American Music: Jazz and its Ancestors

During the 1920s, Harlem was becoming a fashionable place for white people to go. White New Yorkers and tourists went "uptown" to Harlem nightclubs to listen to jazz, probably the greatest artistic achievement of Black Americans. The black people who lived in Harlem and the owners of the nighclubs had every reason to resent the whites, but they were profiting so much from the business that everyone seemed to get along.

Jazz did not suddenly appear in the 1920s. It was part of a tradition of Black American music going back to slavery times—back even further than that, to the rhythms and melodies of Africa. Along the way, elements of other forms of American and European music were added.

Singing, dancing, and playing musical instruments as a means of expression was common in Africa among peoples of many nations. It was one way that people of different tribes could communicate with one another, and one part of African life that survived the years of slavery. In fact, singing was encouraged by the slave owners, who foolishly assumed that music would keep the slaves' minds off their misery.

The first great musical form developed by Black Americans was the *spiritual.* Spirituals

(Text continues on page 49.)

Three Poems by Langston Hughes

Dream Deferred

What happens to a dream deferred?
Does it dry up
like a raisin in the sun?
Or fester like a sore—
And then run?
Does it stink like rotten meat?
Or crust and sugar over—
like a syrupy sweet?

Maybe it just sags
like a heavy load.

Or does it explode?

Motto

I play it cool
And dig all jive—
That's the reason
I stay alive.

My motto,
As I live and learn
Is
Dig and be dug
In return.

I, Too, Sing America

I, too, sing America.

I am the darker brother.
They send me to eat in the kitchen
When company comes,
But I laugh,
And eat well,
And grow strong.

Tomorrow,
I'll be at the table
When company comes.
Nobody'll dare
Say to me,
"Eat in the kitchen,"
Then.

Besides,
They'll see how beautiful I am
And be ashamed—

I, too, am America.

Three Spirituals

Motherless Child

Sometimes I feel like a motherless child,
Sometimes I feel like a motherless child,
Sometimes I feel like a motherless child,
A long ways from home,
A long ways from home.

Sometimes I feel like I'm almost gone,
Sometimes I feel like I'm almost gone,
Sometimes I feel like I'm almost gone,
A long way from home,
A long way from home.

Sometimes I feel like a feather in the air,
Sometimes I feel like a feather in the air,
Sometimes I feel like a feather in the air,
And I spread my wings and I fly.
I spread my wings and I fly.

Go Tell It on the Mountain

Go tell it on the mountain,
Over the hills and everywhere;
Go tell it on the mountain,
That Jesus Christ is born.

When I was a seeker
I sought both night and day,
I asked the Lord to help me
And he showed me the way.

He made me a watchman
Upon a city wall,
And if I am a Christian
I am the least of all.

Go tell it on the mountain,
Over the hills and everywhere;
Go tell it on the mountain,
That Jesus Christ is born.

Go Down, Moses

When Israel was in Egyptland
Let my people go
Oppressed so hard they could not stand
Let my people go.

Go down, Moses,
Way down in Egyptland
Tell old Pharaoh,
"Let my people go."

"Thus saith the Lord," bold Moses said,
"Let my people go,
If not I'll smite your firstborn dead,
Let my people go!"

Go down, Moses,
Way down in Egyptland,
Tell old Pharaoh,
"Let my people go."

Black Americans: Reading Comprehension   No. 2412

were religious songs which sang of a love for Jesus and a desire for heaven. (By the 1800s, most of the slaves were native-born Americans who had taken on the Christian religion of their masters.) In many spirituals, death is seen as a release from the hell of slavery. "Free at last," one spiritual sings of death, "Thank God Almighty, I'm free at last!" The spirituals sang of freedom, hard trials ("Nobody knows the trouble I've seen"), and the grief of being separated from loved ones. Some spirituals told of the everyday life of the people. Slaves used them to tell each other about the Underground Railroad and other important things. "Follow the drinking gourd," says one such song, "For the old man is a—waitin' for to carry you to freedom." The "drinking gourd" was what slaves called the stars of the Big Dipper—a guide that was used by slaves escaping to the North.

Spirituals also gave birth to the lively *gospel* music heard in many black churches, and to the form of music known as *the blues.* Blues are usually songs of troubles and hardship. They are usually slow and sad, but they can also sound lively and cheerful, even when the words tell of poverty and loneliness. A more modern form known as "urban blues" is far louder and more aggressive, and is one of the forms of music that influenced the first rock-'n'-roll musicians in the 1950s.

One of the most famous of the early blues singers was Blind Lemon Jefferson. In the 1920s, Bessie Smith was known as "Queen of the blues." The most famous blues composer of all was

W.C. Handy. He wrote over 60 blues pieces, including the famous "St. Louis Blues," "Memphis Blues," and "Beale Street Blues." Other great blues musicians of yesterday and today include Ma Rainey, Muddy Waters, B.B. King, Mississippi John Hurt, Big Joe Turner, Willie Dixon, Howlin' Wolf, Sonny Boy Williamson, Alberta Hunter, Josh White, and Linda Hopkins. (Again, you don't have to memorize the names of these musicians, but you might enjoy listening to some of their records.)

A Few Blues Verses

Sometimes I feel like nothin', somethin' throwed away
Sometimes I feel like nothin', something throwed away
Then I get my guitar and play the blues all day.

Money's all gone, I'm so far from home
Money's all gone, I'm so far from home
I just sit here and cry and moan.

Good lookin' woman make a bulldog break his chain
Good lookin' woman make a bulldog break his chain
Good lookin' woman make a snail catch a passenger train.

I'm awful lonesome, all alone and blue
I'm awful lonesome, all alone and blue
Ain't got nobody to tell my troubles to.

The end of slavery and the migration to the North brought changes to the lives of Black Americans. Music that expressed the experiences and feelings of the older days was no longer enough. The new freedom and new ways of making a living called for and inspired a new kind of music: *ragtime.*

Ragtime was popular between about 1890 and 1920. It differed from earlier forms of Black American music in that it was actually written down, not simply passed on from one musician to another. At first ragtime was written only for the piano, but later, composers started writing it for groups of instruments.

What makes ragtime different from other music? The person playing the piano uses a different kind of beat for each hand. The left hand keeps regular time, while the right hand goes faster and seems to be sort of bouncy. The best way to understand it is to listen to it. Many records are available of the music of ragtime composers, expecially the greatest of them all, Scott Joplin. He was the son of two musicians in Sedalia, Missouri, and later lived and worked in St. Louis. Two of his best-known pieces are "The Maple Leaf" and "The Entertainer." But Joplin did not think of himself as just a writer of

Scott Joplin　　　　*Louis Armstrong*　　　　*Duke Ellington*

songs. He considered ragtime to be a permanent and serious branch of classical music. He even composed a ragtime opera, *Treemonisha,* which was not performed until more than 60 years after his death in 1917.

Ragtime began to lose its popularity around 1920, partly because of imitators who cheapened the art. By then, elements of both ragtime and the blues had been borrowed by black musicians who played in the new style: jazz.

Jazz is believed to have begun in and around the city of New Orleans in the 1890s. By 1920 it had taken root in Kansas City, Chicago, Washington, D.C., New York and other cities. It soon spread around the world. In such far-away places as Russia, Japan, Australia, and South America, jazz is known as *the* American music. A few white Americans and foreign-born musicians have made important contributions to jazz. But jazz was a Black American invention, and its leading artists have always been Black Americans.

The 1920s were called the jazz age because it was then that jazz was first becoming the most popular form of music in America, as rock 'n' roll is today. The time has also been called the golden age of jazz. Two of the leading musicians of the golden age of jazz (and afterwards) were Louis Armstrong and Duke Ellington.

Being sent to the Waifs' Home for Boys in New Orleans as a child was probably the best thing that could have happened to Louis Armstrong. There he learned to play the cornet (an instrument something like a trumpet). He learned it so well that by the time he was released 18 months later, he was leading a band. He went on to become one of the most important figures in the history of jazz, considered by many to be the world's greatest trumpet player. But it was not only his trumpet playing that brought him fame. He had a wonderful, raspy voice and a sense of comedy that made him a beloved figure. It is sometimes said that Armstrong's genius is what popularized the solo performer in jazz concerts. He also made "scat singing" popular. This is a style in which the singer substitutes nonsense syllables for the words. (Armstrong said he first did it because he forgot the words.) Armstrong seemed to be made for his instrument. His big mouth earned him the nickname "Satchmo" (shortened from "Satchelmouth"), and his strong chest enabled him to really "play that thing!"

If Louis Armstrong invented jazz, as some people say, then Duke Ellington gave it form. Edward Kennedy Ellington invented and perfected his own kind of instrument—the jazz orchestra, or "big band"—and he played it better than anyone. His sound changed as the members of the orchestra changed, because he always looked for ways to develop and show off the individual talents that made up his band.

Ellington is respected not only as a band leader but as a composer. He composed more than 2,000 jazz pieces, including such songs as "It Don't Mean a Thing (If It Ain't Got that Swing)," "Satin Doll," "Mood Indigo," "Sophisticated Lady," and many longer pieces and religious compositions as well. His image was one of elegance and class. Some people consider him the greatest composer, of any kind of music, that America has ever produced.

Armstrong and Ellington were giants, but there have been many other great jazz talents. The list would have to include tenor saxophone players Lester "Prez" Young and Coleman Hawkins, and the greatest alto saxophonest of all time, Charlie "Bird" Parker. Billie Holiday, called "Lady Day," was perhaps the finest singer in the history of jazz. Others on the list of giants would include Dizzy Gillespie, Count Basie, Miles Davis, Ella Fitzgerald, John Coltrane, Thelonius Monk, and today's "young genius of the trumpet," Wynton Marsalis.

Black American Popular Music

Jazz has influenced so many other forms of music that it's sometimes hard to tell where one form ends and another begins. The early spirituals may have inspired the blues, but the spirituals did not disappear. Some of today's great singers such as Aretha Franklin, Ray Charles, and Stevie Wonder, got their start in black religious music. Blues may have melted into jazz, but even today we still have such great blues singers as B.B. King

and Joe Williams. In the 1940s, a new Black American popular music called rhythm and blues first appeared. It had its roots in the spirituals, blues, and jazz, but it was different from all of them. It had a hard-driving, up-tempo beat and was played on amplified instruments such as the electric guitar. "Rhythm and blues" helped give birth to rock 'n' roll in the 1950s and to disco in the 70s. Rhythm and blues has gone through a number of changes and has been known by a number of different names, such as soul music, Motown, and funk. Over the years, its performers have been among the most popular musicians in the world: Chuck Berry, James Brown, the Temptations, Martha Reeves and the Vandellas, Diana Ross, Bill "Smokey" Robinson, Stevie Wonder—and Michael Jackson.

Michael Jackson was very young when he got his start in show business, performing with his four brothers as The Jackson Five. Their break came when they won an amateur talent contest at the famous Apollo Theater in Harlem, the same place where some of the great jazz performers of the past two generations had received their big breaks. The great success of Michael Jackson in the 1980s is not really surprising when you consider how hard he has worked all his life at his singing, his style, and his act. From the earliest days of the Jackson Five, Michael was the show-stealer. When Diana Ross "discovered" him and mentioned the group to Berry Gordy, the founder and president of Motown Records, they were on their way to becoming stars. From then on, they had hit record after hit record.

Since Michael left the Jackson Five for a solo career, his success has been even greater. The peak of his career so far was the 1984 Grammy Awards ceremonies. ("Grammys" are awards given every year for excellence in the recording industry.) Michael received eight Grammys that year, more than any artist in history. Putting a label on his style is very difficult—it's jazz, it's pop, it's rhythm and blues, it's rock. It has certainly had a great influence on the musical style of the 80s.

Michael Jackson

Black Americans: Reading Comprehension   No. 2412

Questions and Activities for Chapter 6

Name _____ Date _____

I. UNDERSTANDING THE WORDS

decades	fashionable	poverty	waifs
century	tradition	aggressive	desire
literature	encouraged	composers	amplified

Fill in the blanks in these sentences using words in the box at the top of the page.

1. _____ are people who write music.

2. Ten _____ make a _____ .

3. _____ are homeless children.

4. Five people in Sonia's family are writers: the creation of _____

   is a _____ in her family.

5. Perhaps because David had grown up in _____ , after he got rich

   he always wore _____ clothes.

6. Ellen got into so many fights that she was suspended from school for her _____

   behavior.

7. The music was _____ enough that we could hear it out on the lawn.

8. Her _____ to become an artist was increased when a famous

   painter saw her work and _____ her to keep working at it.

II. UNDERSTANDING THE FACTS

Match each word or name at the left with the phrase that best describes it. Write the correct letter next to the number.

___ 1. Harlem   A. Black American writer

___ 2. Renaissance   B. leading jazz composer and orchestra leader

___ 3. Langston Hughes   C. famous popular singer of today

___ 4. Jesse B. Semple   D. a French word meaning "rebirth"

___ 5. spirituals   E. a character in short stories

___ 6. blues   F. great blues singer of the 1920s

___ 7. Scott Joplin   G. songs that usually tell of troubles and hardship

___ 8. Bessie Smith   H. religious songs from the days of slavery

___ 9. Duke Ellington   I. the black ghetto of New York City

___ 10. Louis Armstrong   J. great jazz trumpet player and singer

___ 11. Michael Jackson   K. the king of ragtime

III. THOUGHTS OF YOUR OWN

Use a separate sheet of paper to answer these questions.

1. Read the three Langston Hughes poems on page 47. Choose one of them and tell what you think Hughes is talking about in the poem.
2. Read the three spirituals on page 48. Choose one of them and tell what you think the song is about.
3. Do you think that the Harlem Renaissance had much effect on the lives of ordinary Black American men and women? Why or why not?

IV. FOR FAST WORKERS

At your public library, find recordings of black spirituals or of one or more of the blues, jazz, or ragtime musicians mentioned in the chapter. (You can get music by someone who isn't mentioned in the chapter if you like.) Write a one- or two-page report on the music and the musicians.

V. JUST FOR FUN

A. *Here is a list of Black American popular musicians of today and recent years. Copy the list on a separate sheet of paper and write the name of at least one song associated with each performer or group of performers.*

1. Diana Ross	16. Roberta Flack
2. Smokey Robinson	17. Gladys Knight
3. The Temptations	18. Jimi Hendrix
4. The Four Tops	19. Otis Redding
5. Earth, Wind, and Fire	20. Deniece Williams
6. The Jackson Five	21. Richie Havens
7. Michael Jackson	22. Isaac Hayes
8. Sly Stone	23. Lionel Ritchie
9. Aretha Franklin	24. Patrice Rushen
10. James Brown	25. Donna Summer
11. Prince	26. Stevie Wonder
12. Mary Wells	27. Curtis Mayfield
13. Marvin Gaye	28. Chaka Khan
14. Lou Rawls	29. Ray Charles
15. Bill Withers	30. Tina Turner

B. *Here are the names of some Black American actors and actresses. Copy the list on a separate sheet of paper and write the name of at least one movie or TV show that each has performed in.*

1. Sidney Poitier	11. Howard E. Rollins, Jr.
2. Cicely Tyson	12. Michael Warren
3. Kim Fields	13. Paul Winfield
4. Ivan Dixon	14. Ossie Davis
5. Bill Cosby	15. Diahann Carroll
6. Billy Dee Williams	16. Le Var Burton, Jr.
7. Richard Roundtree	17. Diana Ross
8. Ruby Dee	18. Sherman Hemsley
9. Gary Coleman	19. Kevin Hooks
10. Esther Rolle	20. Alfie Woodard

THE YEARS of PROTEST

When World War II broke out in Europe in 1939, the United States began to prepare for war. American factories tooled up to produce planes, guns, tanks, and other war equipment. For white workers, this meant thousands of jobs. But Black Americans did not share in the boom. "Regardless of their training as aircraft workers," said the president of one company, "we will not employ Negroes in our plant. It is against company policy." It was in fact against the policy of nine-tenths of the companies involved in war production.

Black leaders asked President Franklin D. Roosevelt to order an end to racial discrimination in the defense industry. But because he was worried about losing the support of too many whites, especially in the South, Roosevelt would not issue such an order.

Black Americans responded with a new form of protest. A. Philip Randolph, a labor-union organizer, called for a march on Washington to demand an end to job discrimination. The nation's leaders, Randolph said, "will never give the Negro justice until they see masses—ten, twenty, fifty thousand Negroes on the White House lawn."

The march was called for July 1, 1941. As many as 100,000 people were expected to take part. "We shall not call upon our white friends to march with us," Randolph said. "There are some things Negroes must do alone."

Four days before the scheduled march, President Roosevelt issued an order outlawing job discrimination in defense work and creating the Fair Employment Practices Commission (FEPC) to enforce the order. For the next four years, thousands of black men and women were permitted for the first time to work and to be trained for jobs that had always been "for whites only."

But the President's order could only affect *some* jobs, and many employers still found ways to bend the law and keep blacks out. The real importance was in the discovery by Black Americans of their own power to win their rights through protest. The 1941 march on Washington that never took place marked the beginning of what was later to become known as the civil rights movement, the freedom movement, or simply, "The Movement." But it would not really begin to "move" for another 14 years.

A Few Tokens

Meanwhile, a few headline stories gave many white Americans the idea that progress was being made toward equality. Black musicians, entertainers, and sports figures were held up as examples that showed that "anyone could make it in America, regardless of color." Heavyweight boxing champion Joe Louis was called "a credit to his race." Major league baseball accepted its first black players in more than 60 years, starting with Jackie Robinson in 1947. Dr. Ralph Bunche was the U.S. representative to the United Nations and won the Nobel Peace Prize in 1950. Poets Langston Hughes and Gwendolyn Brooks won top national awards for their poetry. Novelist Ralph Ellison won awards for his book *Invisible Man* about a young black man's experiences in the South and in New York. Marian Anderson, a beautiful singer who had started her career in the choir of her church in Philadelphia, joined the Metropolitan Opera Company. But these men and women represented "tokenism," not real progress against racism. For most of America's black citizens, reality was still Jim Crow, urban ghettos, poverty, inferior education, and all the other products of racism.

Still, there was at least the *promise* of change. In May, 1954, the U.S. Supreme Court ruled in the case of *Brown* vs. *Board of Education of Topeka.* It ruled that segregation of the races in schools was against the U.S. Constitution and

would have to stop. The old "separate but equal" idea was held to be false. "Separate educational facilities are inherently unequal," said Chief Justice Earl Warren. The country would have to *integrate* its schools (opposite of *segregate*) "with all deliberate speed."

The *Brown* decision applied only to elementary schools and high schools. But people realized it could also be applied to colleges, libraries, parks, theaters, hotels, and other places. The Supreme Court had spoken. But would the government enforce its ruling? Would white America agree peaceably to it? And just how fast was "with all deliberate speed?"

The Era of Nonviolence

On December 1, 1955, Rosa Parks boarded a bus in Montgomery, Alabama. Under the Jim Crow laws, the first four rows of the bus were reserved for whites only. Mrs. Parks, who was black, took a seat further back. The bus filled up quickly. The driver ordered Mrs. Parks to give up her seat to a white passenger. When she refused, the driver called the police. Mrs. Parks was arrested and taken to jail.

News of her arrest spread quickly through Montgomery's black community. Over the years, many people had been jailed or worse for breaking the segregation laws or for trying to register to vote. This time, though, the community decided to take action. Black leaders called upon the people to boycott the buses— stay off them—until the laws were changed. Perhaps the loss of money from bus fares would pressure the city to change the laws.

An association was formed to organize the

Jackie Robinson   Ralph Bunche   Marian Anderson

Rosa Parks is booked at the Montgomery, Alabama police station.

boycott. The 26-year-old minister who was chosen as its leader set the tone for the boycott when he said, "We are protesting for the birth of justice in our community. In our protest . . . there will be no cross burnings. There will be no threats or intimidation. We will be guided by the highest principles of law and order. . . . Love must be our regulating ideal. In spite of the mistreatment that we have confronted, we must not become bitter and end up by hating our white brothers." The young minister's name was Martin Luther King, Jr.

When he was a college student, Martin Luther King, Jr. had heard a visiting preacher speak on the life and teachings of Mahatma Gandhi. Gandhi had liberated his country, India, from British rule not by armed struggle but through *nonviolent direct action*—massive, peaceful resistance to unjust laws. Gandhi's followers had been jailed and beaten by the thousands; some had been killed. But in the end, they had won— without becoming violent themselves. Could this not be a lesson to Black Americans, King wondered? He recognized that violent resistance to white racism would only bring about further repression. Besides, as a Christian minister, he was guided by Jesus's words, "Love your enemies; bless them that curse you." Might the ideals of Jesus, combined with the practical program of Gandhi, be a plan for the liberation of Black Americans? Could they free themselves

simply by refusing to accept racism? And would they have the determination and courage to remain nonviolent when faced with jail, beatings, or death?

The Montgomery bus boycott lasted a year. During this time King's house was bombed; he and his followers were threatened, harrassed, and jailed. But the boycott held. And at the end of 1956, the Supreme Court struck down Alabama's Jim Crow laws.

Nonviolent direct action had worked. Suddenly Dr. King was the best-known black leader in the United States. His organization, the Southern Christian Leadership Conference (SCLC) asked Black Americans "to assert their human dignity by refusing further cooperation with evil." They would boycott, protest, and picket businesses and institutions that would not accept black and white people as equals. Nonviolence, King reminded his followers, was directed "against forces of evil rather than against people who happen to be doing that evil." The struggle was not between black people and white people but between "justice and injustice."

Martin Luther King, Jr. leads a nonviolent protest march.

With such ideals, Martin Luther King, Jr. became an example to others who sought to win justice and equality for Black Americans. Students in North Carolina desegregated lunch counters simply by sitting down and refusing to leave. The

Police attack demonstrators in Birmingham, Alabama in 1963.

idea of the "sit-in" demonstration spread rapidly. Within two weeks, sit-ins were taking place in 15 southern cities. During the next year, 50,000 people took part in nonviolent sit-ins. They desegregated movie theaters, libraries, parks, and public swimming pools. More than 3,600 people were jailed. Many were beaten, tear-gassed, or shot. But the Jim Crow laws had begun to fall.

An organization called the Congress of Racial Equality (CORE) had quietly and successfully been using nonviolence to fight racism in the North since 1942. Now CORE organizers went south to train demonstrators in discipline and in protecting themselves from clubbing and kicking without fighting back. Another organization, the Student Nonviolent Coordinating Committee (SNCC) was set up with Dr. King's help. They devoted themselves to organized protest and began a drive to help register voters in the South. "Freedom now!" became the slogan of the SNCC and of the whole civil rights movement.

In some parts of the South, whites accepted the fall of Jim Crow calmly, as if they knew it was bound to happen someday. But in other places, reaction was violent. "We want our colored people to go on living like they have for the last 100 years," said a Georgia sheriff in 1961. Martin Luther King, Jr. and his followers were jailed again and again, even though they had broken no laws. Mobs beat up peaceful demonstrators with no interference by police—sometimes with the help of the police. Civil rights workers were murdered; their killers were rarely punished. In

Birmingham, Alabama in 1963, the violence was particularly ugly. Eugene "Bull" Connor, the city's Director of Public Safety, ordered police dogs and fire hoses to be used against marchers, many of whom were children. Four little girls in a Sunday school class were killed when a bomb destroyed a black church.

Millions of Americans watched such events on TV news programs. Faced with the ugliness of racism, many whites who had been hostile or indifferent to black people now became supporters of the Movement. And now, for the first time in more than 80 years, the U.S. government was beginning to enforce the idea of equality. Federal troops were called in when angry mobs tried to block the integration of schools in Arkansas, Mississippi, and Alabama. In 1960, John F. Kennedy was elected President. He met with Martin Luther King, Jr. and other black leaders. His brother, Attorney General Robert Kennedy, used the power of the U.S. Department of Justice to fight segregation in the courts. In 1963, President Kennedy introduced to Congress the first civil rights bill "with teeth" since the days of reconstruction. President Kennedy was assassinated in November of that year, but the new President, Lyndon Johnson, continued to push for the new law. Congress passed the civil rights act in 1964, and a tough voting rights law the following year.

On August 28, 1963, more than 200,000 black and white civil rights marchers assembled in Washington, D.C. They listened to speeches and sang "We Shall Overcome," the song that had become the "national anthem" of the Movement. The chief speaker was Martin Luther King, Jr. His famous "I have a dream" speech, given that day, expressed the hopes of millions of Americans for peace between the races and justice for everyone.

The March on Washington, August 28, 1963.

But for millions of others, it was an empty dream. For many Black Americans, Martin Luther King, Jr., integration, and non-violence offered no solutions to the problem of racism. They looked to other leaders and other methods.

Black Nationalism, Black Rage, Black Power—and Black Pride

For most Black Americans in the big cities of the North and West, the problem wasn't Jim Crow laws and voting rights. Here there was no racism by law, but there was plenty of it in fact. Jobs, housing, and education were the biggest problems. The unemployment rate for blacks was two to three times what it was for whites. Many companies would not hire blacks except for the most menial jobs. Of those black people who did earn a good living, most found that they could not buy houses or rent apartments in "white" neighborhoods. Those who did were sometimes chased out by mobs. They were still concentrated into ghettos, usually in the oldest, shabbiest parts of town. And in most cities, school district lines were drawn to create "black" and "white" schools, as segregated as in the South, and just as unequal.

Poverty, racism, slum living, poor education, unemployment, poverty—it was a vicious cycle. It bred crime, drug abuse, despair and anger. Ghetto residents were exploited by white store owners and brutalized by police. It was no wonder that many Black Americans under these conditions choose to reject intergration. The black man or woman, they reasoned, could never be equal as a member of a minority group in a racist culture. They favored a separate nation for Black Americans, just as Marcus Garvey had talked about 40 years before. If not a separate nation within Africa or the United States, then a completely equal and independent black community.

One well-known black nationalist group was Nation of Islam, also called the Black Muslims. Their leader, Elijah Muhammad, gave black nationalism a religious force. He based his movement on Islam, the dominant religion of the Middle East and of much of Africa. As he saw it, Islam was the "natural religion" for the black man. Black Muslims were forbidden to smoke, drink, or use drugs. They were expected to work hard, study, dress neatly, and stay out of trouble. The Muslims set up their own schools and encouraged their people to shop only at stores owned by other Muslims. As for the white man, Elijah Muhammad taught that he was the devil; his ways were to be avoided.

For many years, the chief spokesman for the Black Muslims was Malcolm X. Born Malcolm Little, he had rejected his family name as a young man. It was a "slave name," he said. The "X" represented his true, African name that had been stolen by the slave traders.

To Malcolm X, nonviolence was a joke. "White people think the black man ought to be shouting 'Hallelujah!,'" Malcolm said of the civil rights movement. "Four hundred years the white man has had his foot-long knife in the black man's back—and now the white man starts to *wiggle* the knife out, maybe six inches. The black man's supposed to be grateful? Why, if white man *jerked* the knife out, it's still going to leave a *scar!*"

Malcolm X

Malcolm X often spoke about violence in America. In one speech, he said, "If it is wrong to be violent defending black women and black children and black babies and black men, then it is wrong for America to draft us [into the army] and make us violent in defense of her. And if it is right for America to draft us . . . then it is right for you and me to do whatever is necessary to defend our people right here in this country."

Malcolm's anger and the power of his words drew many supporters who were not Muslims. Even Martin Luther King, Jr. told a friend, "When [Malcolm] starts talking about all that's been done to us, I get a twinge of hate, of identification with him."

In 1964, Malcolm traveled to the Middle East and Africa. What he discovered there changed his way of thinking. True Islam, it seemed, did not preach that the white man was a devil. It taught that all men were brothers. The white man was not evil, Malcolm now told his people, "but America's racist society influences him to act evilly." Malcolm broke with the Black Muslims. He began telling his audiences, "I don't speak against [all] white people. . . . I have learned that not all white people are racists. I am speaking against, and my fight is against, the white *racists.*" Malcolm had barely begun to work for what he called "an honest black-white brotherhood" when he was murdered while giving a speech in New York in February, 1965. Three black men, two of them Black Muslims, were convicted of his murder and sent to prison.

The anger Malcolm expressed was felt by many. It boiled over in the ghettos between 1964 and 1968. In New York, Los Angeles, Detroit, Cleveland, Chicago, Newark—in dozens of cities, large and small, violent rebellions broke out and raged for several days. In most cases they were triggered by reported acts of brutality by police. Rioters fought with police and burned and looted ghetto stores owned by whites. Hundreds of people died, most of them ghetto residents; thousands were arrested, millions of dollars in property was destroyed or stolen.

The rebellions in the ghettos alerted white America to the rage that many blacks were

A ghetto street in Chicago after the riot of April, 1968.

Black Americans: Reading Comprehension   No. 2412

feeling. A commission appointed by President Johnson came to the not-surprising conclusion that white racism lay at the core of black rage. Martin Luther King turned his efforts to the North. He led marches in support of job opportunities for blacks in New York and for fair housing in Chicago. But he found hatred and anger among whites that was worse than anything he has experienced in the South, and he was heckled and jeered by blacks. The civil rights movement was dead, as many people saw it. Instead, a "black revolution" was taking place. Younger black leaders like Stokeley Carmichael of SNCC and Roy Innes of CORE were now speaking of "black power" instead of civil rights. "This country don't run on love, brother," said the fiery young Carmichael. "It runs on power, and we ain't got none."

The people who spoke the words "black power" were mostly young blacks who felt that the fight against racism was being held up by white support, by "integration" on the white man's terms. The very idea of integration, they felt, was racist. To be "integrated," they felt, meant that Black Americans were being told to reject their own culture. "Brothers and sisters, don't let them separate you from other black people," Carmichael said. "Don't ever in your life apologize for your black brothers. Don't be ashamed of your culture, because if you have no culture you don't exist. . . . Don't ever, don't ever, don't ever be ashamed of being black."

Still, many people were convinced that black power did mean violence, especially after SNCC dropped the word "nonviolent" from its name. If there was any doubt that the civil rights movement was dead, there was none after April 4, 1968. On that day, Martin Luther King, Jr. was shot dead in Memphis, Tennessee by a white, small-time hoodlum named James Earl Ray. Even today, questions remain about whether someone "put him up to it."

Even more militant than Stokeley Carmichael and his followers were the Black Panther Party for Self-Defense. The Panthers admired Malcolm X and other black nationalists, but they were more radical in their ideas. Their ten-point program called for complete control of the black community *by* the black community, including schools, police power, and the economy. They demanded money from the U.S. government for

the black community as repayment for slavery. They demanded freedom for all black prisoners, because they saw them as not having received a fair trial. Black prisoners, they said, should be tried by black juries. In the ghettos, the Panthers set up free health clinics, a free breakfast program for children, and free schools for the teaching of black history and culture. They demanded an end to police brutality, started self-defense groups, and fought back when attacked by police.

The Panthers won a great deal of support in the ghettos. Even many whites, particularly college students, openly admired the militancy of the Panthers. But of course fighting the police was a losing battle. Panther leaders were jailed, mostly on charges later proven to be false. Panthers were gunned down by police, some in cold blood. Panther leader Eldridge Cleaver left the country to avoid going to prison, where he feared he would be killed by guards. Meanwhile, many blacks were becoming less militant. By 1972, the Black Panther Party had all but disappeared.

Out of all the turmoil of the civil rights and

black power movements came a new sense of pride among Black Americans. In some ways they had moved closer to equality with whites, but they also had come to realize that "black is beautiful." Schools and colleges began programs in black studies. Black Americans rediscovered their own history, literature, and culture. Some converted to Islam, as practiced not by the Black Muslims but by the Muslims of the Middle East. There was a growth of interest in Africa and its peoples. Many Black Americans took on African names, wore Afriican clothes, and visited the lands of their ancestors. They were finding pride in their culture, as the black-power leaders had urged.

Alex Haley was a black writer who had worked with Malcolm X on his autobiography. While growing up in Tennessee, he had heard his grandmother and aunts tell stories about their family going back to slavery days, back to an ancestor they called "the African." With the help of these stories, some hard work, and a lot of luck, Haley found the very village in which his great-great-great-great grandfather had been born more than 200 years before. His book *Roots,* about his African ancestors and his search for them, became a source of pride for all Black Americans when it came out in 1976. The TV production of *Roots* was watched by the largest audience in the history of television up to that time.

Questions and Activities for Chapter 7

Name _____ Date _____

I. UNDERSTANDING THE WORDS

A. *All the words in the box below can be found hidden in the puzzle. Find and circle each word. They may be written horizontally, vertically, or diagonally, and either forward or backward. When you've finished the puzzle, use a separate sheet of paper to write a sentence for each of the words.*

regardless	confronted	exploited	commission
inherently	picket	influences	advocating
register	indifferent	convicted	autobiography
intimidation	unemployment		

```
C O N F R O N T E D W F R A R R O W F V
I W L D A P N M L S C T L V E V U E V P
U G W M D G R W K H O Q J P G A I I T X
W A Z B V A R W A R M Y K J A U W Z W V
U P K B O T U X G W M J C F R Z S W R O
G I Y Q C E K T G O I Y A E D C F L T U
Z B N V A U A K O Y S U U G L Q I C F G
I K O T T Q G L O B S D E J E P Q O V I
Z N Y H I I B T B N I Y R Q S I K N R N
L B D S N M C L Z H O O H Z S C Q V E H
Y N G I G E I L I C N F G E E K I I G E
I B V Y F T X D F L K X Z R F E B C I R
J U E X U F B P A V L U X J A T W T S E
A E L O H S E X L T E A S D Z P T E T N
Y H A B L R R R G O I Z H E K E H D E T
X J B M Z S R W E X I O P H N S M Y R L
V T X E Y T F S G N I T N F E D L P K Y
I N F L U E N C E S T U E M Y Y I A O O
V W V O D Q P S N Y Y T D D N V S J Y S
C V U Y N K V U N E M P L O Y M E N T B
```

B. *Be a word detective!* The word *boycott* was originally a person's name. Use a dictionary and encyclopedia to find out who he was and how his name came to be a word meaning *a protest by avoidance.* Use a separate sheet of paper to write a paragraph explaining it.

Black Americans: Reading Comprehension   No. 2412

II. UNDERSTANDING THE FACTS

Circle the letter of the word or phrase that best completes each sentence.

1. A. Philip Randolph organized a march on Washington, D.C. by Black Americans to protest
   a) for the right to vote.   b) against lynchings.   c) against job discrimination.

2. The march on Washington, D.C.
   a) took place on July 1, 1941.   b) did not take place for 14 years.   c) did not take place at all.

3. _____ was a heavyweight boxing champion.
   a) Joe Louis   b) Jackie Robinson   c) Ralph Ellison

4. _____ won a top national award for poetry.
   a) Marian Anderson   b) Gwendolyn Brooks   c) Ralph Bunche

5. *Brown* vs. *Board of Education of Topeka* was a Supreme Court decision against segregation in
   a) schools.   b) baseball.   c) jobs.

6. Martin Luther King, Jr. first became well known for leading
   a) a march on Washington.   b) a protest against segregated schools.
   c) a boycott of segregated buses.

7. King's method of nonviolent direct action came from the life and teachings of
   a) Booker T. Washington.   b) Mahatma Gandhi.   c) Earl Warren.

8. The "sit-in" demonstrations began in
   a) North Carolina.   b) Washington, D.C.   c) New York City.

9. SNCC was an abbreviation for
   a) Student Nonviolent Coordinating Committee.
   b) Southern Nonviolent Community Conference.   c) Southern Negro Christian Committee.

10. Eugene "Bull" Connor turned police dogs on protest marchers in
   a) Birmingham, Alabama.   b) Montgomery, Alabama.   c) Philadelphia, Mississippi.

11. _____ was President when the 1964 civil rights law was passed.
   a) John F. Kennedy   b) Lyndon Johnson   c) Richard Nixon

12. At the March on Washington in 1963, _____ gave his famous "I have a dream" speech.
   a) Philip Randolph   b) Martin Luther King, Jr.   c) Malcolm X

13. Elijah Muhammad was
   a) a black nationalist and religious leader.   b) a champion boxer.
   c) the head of an African state.

14. Malcolm X was a leading spokesman for
   a) the NAACP.   b) the SCLC.   c) the Black Muslims.

15. The "X" in Malcolm's name
   a) was the initial of an African name that was too hard to pronounce.
   b) represented his unknown African name.   c) was a name given to him in prison.

16. Malcolm X change his views on white people after
   a) President Kennedy was assassinated.
   b) his trip to the Middle East.   c) he met and talked with Martin Luther King, Jr.

17. Anger over racism led to _____ between 1964 and 1968.
   a) rioting in the ghettos   b) black control of the ghettos   c) marches for voting rights

18. "Black power" was a slogan used by _____ and his followers.

          a) Martin Luther King, Jr.   b) Malcolm X   c) Stokeley Carmichael

19. When people used the phrase "black power," they were usually talking about

          a) returning to Africa.   b) violence.   c) political power.

20. _____ was a leader of the Black Panther Party.

          a) Malcolm X   b) Eldridge Cleaver   c) Alex Haley

21. The Panthers were in favor of

          a) black control of the black community.

          b) fighting back when attacked by police.   c) both a and b.

22. The Panthers were not able to set up _____ in the ghettos.

          a) free schools and clinics   b) a black-controlled police force   c) breakfast programs for children

23. One thing that came out of the black power movement was

          a) equality for blacks.   b) an end to prejudice in the North.

          c) a new sense of pride among Black Americans.

24. Alex Haley helped _____ write his autobiography.

          a) Martin Luther King, Jr.   b) Malcolm X   c) Eldridge Cleaver

25. Haley's book, *Roots,* was about

          a) his search for his African ancestors.

          b) the black power movement.   c) growing up in Tennessee.

III. THOUGHTS OF YOUR OWN

Use a separate sheet of paper to answer these questions.

1. The 1941 march on Washington never took place. Why do you think the President gave in to the demands of the march leaders rather than having it take place?
2. Boxing champion Joe Louis was called "a credit to his race." What do you think white people meant by this? Do you think black people thought of it as a compliment or an insult? Why?
3. Why do you think Martin Luther King, Jr.'s method of nonviolent direct action was more effective in the South than in the North?
4. The "black power" people thought that integration with whites meant that black people were being asked to reject their own culture. Do you agree? Why or why not?
5. Martin Luther King, Jr., Malcolm X, Stokeley Carmichael, and the black Panthers all had different ideas about how to combat racism. Which way do you think worked the best? Which do you think was the least effective? Give reasons for your answers.

IV. FOR FAST WORKERS

Write a one- or two-page report about one of the Black Americans mentioned in this chapter or on one of those listed below. Use your school or public library to find the information.

Medgar Evers, *civil rights leader*

Fannie Lou Hamer, *civil rights leader*

Paul Robeson, *actor/singer*

Maya Angelou, *writer/composer/actress*

Calvin Simmons, *musician*

Nikki Giovanni, *poet*

Judith Jamison, *dancer*

John H. Johnson, *publisher*

Berry Gordy, *businessman*

Leontyne Price, *singer*

Andre Watts, *pianist*

Althea Gibson, *tennis player*

Alice Walker, *writer*

Gregory Hines, *dancer*

Chapter 8

FREEDOM WHEN?

So what happened? Did the civil rights movement, the rebellions in the ghettos, and black power make Black Americans any freer? Is there equality between black and white Americans today? Are we any closer to it than we were 30 years ago?

Good News, Bad News

The answers to those questions are: yes, no, and maybe. For a start, Jim Crow is dead— almost. It is rare to find any public place that is not open equally to blacks and whites. Segregation has almost disappeared from hotels, restaurants, parks, and entertainment places. As far as that goes, the civil rights movement was a success.

But education is a different story. Hundreds of thousands more black students now attend desegregated schools than did in 1954, but most black children still attend schools that are "separate and unequal." Since 1970 there has been a tremendous increase in the number of black students who graduate from high school and go on to college and beyond. But today, more than 30 years after the Supreme Court's *Brown* decision, there is still a large "education gap" between black and white Americans.

No type of job today is closed to Black Americans. There are far more black lawyers, construction workers, office workers, salespersons, news reporters, teachers, skilled factory workers, police officers, bank officers, government officials, and business executives than threre were in the 1960s. In most cities, any black person who has the money can buy a home or rent an apartment in neighborhoods that 20 years ago were "white only." As far as that goes, the protest marches, rebellions, lawsuits, and civil rights laws led to real progress.

But blacks still lag far behind other Americans in income. The unempolyment rate for blacks is still twice that for whites. While Black Americans may have an equal chance at any job for

Barbara Jordan
(former congresswoman, national leader)

Shirley Chisholm
(first black congresswoman)

Gordon Parks
(photographer, composer, and filmmaker)

which they are qualified, many have been handicapped by poor education. In many businesses and professions, blacks seem to be able to rise to a certain level—and no further. Despite laws against discrimination there are still neighborhoods where blacks are kept from buying or renting property. And while many Black Americans have "moved uptown," many more are still in the ghetto. There is concern that a "permanent underclass" is forming in America, of people never able to find steady work and living lives dependent on government welfare programs.

Dozens of American cities are today governed by black mayors. There are thousands of black lawyers, judges, and government executives in office around the country. Politicians must consider the needs and interests of black voters. As far as that goes, black power had been achieved.

But most Black Americans are far from having control over their lives and communities. Black Americans have relatively little voice at the highest levels of power. There are places where the Ku Klux Klan and other racist groups are still feared. And some politicians have tried (unsuccessfully) to stop enforcement of important civil rights and voting rights laws.

Some real changes did come out of the years of protest. Black Americans have achieved the dignity fought for by Frederick Douglass, Harriet Tubman, W.E.B. Du Bois, Martin Luther King, Jr., Malcolm X, and others. Many Black Americans today can and do live without daily insults and reminders of second-class citizenship. The ugly destructiveness of racism has not gone away, but far more whites have come to see blacks not as outsiders, tokens, or "Negroes" but as individual human beings. When Guion S. Bluford, Jr. went into orbit aboard the space shuttle in 1983, few newspapers made any fuss about his being America's first black astronaut—he was simply an astronaut. Atlanta's mayor Andrew Young and former Texas congresswoman Barbara Jordan are seen not only as black leaders, but as national leaders. It's hard for many white Americans to remain racists when they are treated by a black doctor, buy shoes from a black store clerk, watch a black reporter deliver the news on TV, and see black people in commercials enjoying the same products they use.

And it works both ways. Even the Black

Muslims have stopped preaching that the white man is the devil. They have moved closer in their teaching to the beliefs of Muslims around the world.

But Black Americans are still not really close to equality with whites. Some people feel that they do have *equality of opportunity*—that the laws are in place that will bring about equality after some time has passed. But other people don't believe it. "After some time has passed" is a promise Black Americans have heard before. Many believe that it will take another "push" such as happened in the 1960s to bring about equal opportunity.

Some Hot issues

In the area of education, some cities desegregate their schools by sending children by bus to schools in other neighborhoods. The Supreme Court has ruled that schools must be desegregated, and that it is legal for cities or counties to require busing if that's what it takes. In many places, busing goes on peacefully. But in others, people have angrily fought the idea of forced busing. In some places there has been violence over busing. In others, parents have taken children out of the school system. The family either moves or sends their children to private schools. Many black parents as well as others don't like sending their children on long bus rides instead of to neighborhood schools. No one has come up with an easy answer to the problem. Meanwhile many children are still going to schools that are separate and unequal.

Another hot issue is *affirmative action*. When hiring someone for a job, it's aganst the law to discriminate on the basis of race or sex. (You may have seen job advertisements that say "an equal opportunity employer.") Affirmative action goes a step further. It's a plan that says that employers should make a special effort to hire women and members of minority groups. Many people don't like the idea of affirmative action, and others think it doesn't go far enough. They feel that there can never be true equality unless there are *quotas* for hiring. Since 11 percent of the American people are black, the people who favor quotas say that 11 percent of the jobs should go to blacks—even if someone else is better qualified. In the years to come, there will be a great deal of arguing over the question of affirmative action and quotas.

Leontyne Price
(world famous singer)

Andrew Young
(congressman, ambassador, and mayor)

Alice Walker
(prize-winning writer)

Following New Leaders, Honoring Old Ones

Since the 1970s, Black Americans have had a real voice in government for the first time in our history. Blacks no longer have to depend only on protest marches to get the government to listen to them. At the national level, blacks in the U.S. House of Representatives have organized the Congressional Black Caucus. This group works to pass laws that are of interest to Black Americans. It also keeps an eye on how the government is enforcing laws against discrimination. Black mayors have been elected (and in many cases re-elected) in Gary, Indiana; Fayette, Mississippi; Cleveland; Philadelphia; Los Angeles; Atlanta; Chicago; Washington, D.C., and other cities. Mayor Tom Bradley of Los Angeles came within just a few thousand votes of being elected Governor of California, the nation's largest state, in 1982.

But In 1984, the Black American leader with the greatest national following was clearly the Reverend Jesse Jackson. A Baptist minister from South Carolina, Jackson became active in the civil rights movement as a young man. He became a close associate of Martin Luther King, Jr. and was with Dr. King when he was killed. Jackson moved to Chicago, where he organized two important community projects. Operation Breadbasket was a program to feed hungry people in the ghetto, and PUSH (People United to Save Humanity) was a program to win control for blacks of their own community and equal opportunity in the larger community. The key to Jackson's program was *self-help*: Black Americans improving themselves by their own efforts; through the notion that "I am somebody."

In 1984, Jackson was a candidate for the Democratic Party's nomination for President of the United States. Hundreds of thousands of Black Americans who had never bothered to register to vote—what was the point?—now registered so that they could vote for Jackson. Although Jackson did not get the nomination, he did get the support of some non-black voters. While some of his statements made a great many people angry, his campaign showed America the growing political strength of its black citizens. Jackson's speech at the 1984 Democratic convention was seen by millions of Americans on television.

But other leaders are not forgotten. In 1983, Congress made January 15 a national holiday honoring the birthday of Martin Luther King, Jr. In a way though, the holiday honors more than Dr. King's birthday. It is also a day of honor for all Black Americans—a recognition by the United States, at last, of its black citizens and their 400 years of contributions to America.

Jesse Jackson

Questions and Activities for Chapter 8

Name _____ Date _____

I. UNDERSTANDING THE WORDS

Circle the letter of the answer that means the same as the underlined word in each sentence. Use a dictionary if you need help.

1. There are many more black business <u>executives</u> today than there were 30 years ago.
   a) owners   b) managers   c) teachers

2. Some people think there should be <u>quotas</u> for hiring Black Americans to fill jobs.
   a) rules   b) shares according to numbers   c) special committees

3. Jesse Jackson was an <u>associate</u> of Martin Luther King, Jr.
   a) fellow worker or partner   b) good friend   c) enemy

4. Jackson ran for the Democratic Party's <u>nomination</u> for President.
   a) official naming as a candidate   b) election   c) advisor

5. There is concern that a <u>permanent</u> underclass is forming in America.
   a) temporary   b) continuing or enduring   c) segregated

6. Black Americans have achieved the <u>dignity</u> fought for by Frederick Douglass and others.
   a) financial rewards   b) self-respect and pride   c) independence

7. The key to Jackson's program was self-help: Black Americans improving themselves by their own efforts; through the <u>notion</u> that "I am somebody."
   a) belief   b) uncertainty   c) untruth

II. UNDERSTANDING THE FACTS

Circle T if the answer is true. Circle F if the answer is false.

T F   1. Jim Crow laws have almost disappeared.

T F   2. Most black children now attend integrated schools.

T F   3. There are still almost no black lawyers or news reporters.

T F   4. Several large American cities have black mayors.

T F   5. The Ku Klux Klan no longer exists.

T F   6. Most people agree that busing and affirmative action are good ideas.

T F   7. Tom Bradley was almost elected Governor of New York in 1982.

T F   8. Jesse Jackson was the organizer of PUSH and Operation Breadbasket.

T F   9. Jesse Jackson's candidacy encouraged many Black Americans to register to vote for the first time.

T F 10. The nation celebrates Martin Luther King's birthday on February 15.

T F 11. *Affirmative action* is a plan for making a special effort to hire women and minorities.

T F 12. Guion S. Bluford is a highly respected journalist.

T F 13. All Americans now favor voting rights laws.

T F 14. The Congressional Black Caucus is a group of black members of the House of Representatives.

T F 15. *Equality of opportunity* means that everyone has the same chance to succeed.

T F 16. The Supreme Court has ruled that only schools in the South are required by law to be desegregated.

III. THOUGHTS OF YOUR OWN

You have now completed the final chapter of **Black Americans—From Africa to the 80's.** *On the lines below, list several facts you were surprised to learn about Black American history. Then use a separate sheet of paper to answer the questions that follow.*

_____

_____

_____

_____

_____

_____

_____

_____

_____

_____

_____

_____

_____

_____

_____

1. What do you think it would take to bring about *real* equality between blacks and whites in America?
2. Do you think such programs as affirmative action are fair? Give reasons for your answer.
3. The number of blacks in the U.S. Congress is still quite small. Do you think they can really make a difference in the kinds of laws that are passed and the way the laws are enforced? Give reasons for your answer.
4. Do you agree that the holiday honoring Martin Luther King, Jr.'s birthday is also a day honoring all Black Americans? Why or why not?

IV. FOR FAST WORKERS

Match each Black American political leader with the office he or she holds or has held recently. Write the correct letter next to each number.

____ 1. Shirley Chisholm   A. Mayor—Philadelphia, Pennsylvania

____ 2. Barbara Jordan   B. Senator—Massachusetts

____ 3. Ronald V. Dellums   C. Congressperson-Georgia

____ 4. Tom Bradley   D. Congressperson—New York

____ 5. Wilson Goode   E. Mayor—Los Angeles, California

____ 6. Coleman Young   F. Mayor—Gary, Indiana

____ 7. Julian Bond   G. Justice—U.S. Supreme Court

____ 8. Thurgood Marshall   H. Mayor—Detroit, Michigan

____ 9. Richard Hatcher   I. Congressperson—Texas

____ 10. Edward Brooke   J. Congressperson—California

For Further Reading

This is a general bibliography. It includes books that will be of interest to students from the middle grades on up through high school and also books intended for adult reading. Subject matter of the book is indicated except where the title make it self-explanatory.

Abdul, Raoul. *Famous Black Entertainers of Today.* Dodd, 1974.
Adoff, Arnold. *Black on Black: Commentaries by Negro Americans.* Harper, 1973.
Adoff, Arnold. *The Poetry of Black America: Anthology of the 20th Century.* Harper, 1973.
Ali, Muhammad. *The Greatest: My Own Story.* Random, 1975.
Angelou, Maya. *Gather Together In My Name.* Random, 1974; autobiography.
Angelou, Maya. *I Know Why the Caged Bird Sings.* Random, 1970; autobiography.
Angelou, Maya. *Singin' and Swingin' and Gettin' Merry like Christmas.* Random, 1979; autobiography.
Aptheker, Herbert. *American Negro Slave Revolts.* International Publishing Co., 1983.
Ashe, Arthur. *Arthur Ashe: Portrait in Motion.* Houghton, 1975; autobiography.

Baldwin, James. *The Fire Next Time.* Watts, 1963; essays.
Baldwin, James. *Go Tell It On the Mountain.* Dial, 1963; fiction.
Bambara, Toni Cade, ed. *Tales and Stories for Black Folk.* Zenith, 1971; fiction.
Bartol, Roland. *Sundiata: The Epic of the Lion King.* Crowell, 1970; African heroic legend retold for younger readers.
Bennett, Lerone, Jr. *Before the Mayflower.* Johnson, 1969; history.
Bennett, Lerone, Jr. *What Manner of Man?* Johnson, 1968; biography of Martin Luther King, Jr.
Bontemps, Arna. *Anyplace But Here.* Hill, 1966; history.
Bradford, Sarah E. *Harriet Tubman, the Moses of Her People.* Peter Smith, 1961.
Brooks, Gwendolyn. *Bean Eaters.* Harper, 1960; poetry.
Brooks, Gwendolyn. *In the Mecca.* Harper, 1968; poetry.
Brookter, Marie. *Here I Am—Take My Hand.* Harper, 1974; autobiography.
Brown, Claude. *Manchild in the Promised Land.* Random, 1968; autobiography.

Carmichael, Stokeley. *Black Power.* Random, 1968.
Chapman, Abraham. *New Black Voices.* New American Library, 1973; prose and poetry anthology.
Childress, Alice. *A Hero Ain't Nothin' But a Sandwich.* Avon, 1982; fiction.
Chisholm, Shirley. *Unbought and Unbossed.* Houghton, 1970; autobiography.
Cleaver, Eldridge. *Soul on Ice.* McGraw-Hill, 1968; essays.
Conot, Robert E. *Rivers of Blood, Years of Darkness.* Morrow, 1967; study of 1965 Watts riot.

David, Jay, ed. *Growing Up Black.* Morrow, 1968; anthology of autobiographical sketches.
Davidson, Basil. *The African Past.* Little, Brown, 1964.
Davidson, Basil. *Lost Cities of Africa.* Little, Brown, 1959.
Douglass, Frederick. *The Life and Times of Frederick Douglass.* Grosset, 1970.
Du Bois, W.E.B. *The Souls of Black Folk .* Dodd, 1970; essays.
Du Bois, W.E.B. *Black Folk, Then and Now.* Kraus Reprints, 1975; essays.
Durham, Philip, and E.L. Jones. *Negro Cowboys.* Dodd, 1965.

Ebony, eds. *Black Revolution.* Johnson, 1970; essays.
Ellison, Ralph. *Invisible Man.* Random, 1952; fiction.
Evans, Mari. *I Am a Black Woman.* Morrow, 1970; poetry.

Feelings, Tom. *Black Pilgrimage .* Lothrop, 1972; black artist's account of a trip to Africa.
Fishel, Leslie, and B. Quarles. *The Black American: A Documentary History.* Scott, Foresman, 1976.
Franklin, John Hope. *From Slavery to Freedom: A History of American Negroes.* Knopf, 1980, 5th edition.
Frazier, Walt. *Rockin' Steady: A Guide to Basketball and Cool.* Prentice-Hall, 1974.

Gaines, Ernest J. *The Autobiography of Miss Jane Pittman.* Doubleday, 1971; fiction.
Giovanni, Nikki. *Black Feeling, Black Talk, Black Judgment.* Morrow, 1968; poetry.
Giovanni, Nikki. *Spin a Soft Black Song: Poems for Children.* Morrow, 1971.
Goldston, Robert. *The Negro Revolution.* Macmillan, 1968.
Grant, Joanne. *Black Protest: History, Documents, and an Analysis from 1619 to the Present.* Fawcett, 1972.
Gregory, Dick. *Nigger.* Dutton, 1964; autobiography.
Greene, Bette. *Philip Hall Likes Me . . . I Reckon, Maybe.* Dell, 1975; fiction.
Greenfield, Eloise. *Mary McLeod Bethune.* Harper, 1977; biography.
Guy, Rosa. *The Friends.* Bantom, 1983; fiction.

Haley, Alex. *Roots.* Doubleday, 1976; family history as novel.
Harris, Janet. *Black Pride: A People's Struggle.* McGraw-Hill, 1969.
Hamilton, Virginia. *Paul Robeson.* Harper, 1974; biography.
Hamilton, Virginia, ed. *The Writings of W.E.B. Du Bois.* Crowell, 1975.
Hansberry, Lorraine. *A Raisin in the Sun.* Random, 1959; play.
Haskins, James. *Fighting Shirley Chisholm.* Dial, 1975.
Haskins, James. *Ralph Bunche: A Most Reluctant Hero.* Hawthorn, 1974.
Hughes, Langston. *A Pictorial History of Black Americans.* Crown, 1973.
Hughes, Langston, ed. *The Best Short Stories by Negro Writers.* Little, Brown, 1967.
Hughes, Langston, and Arna Bontemps, eds. *Book of Negro Folklore.* Dodd, 1958.

Jackson, Florence. *Blacks in America, 1954-1979.* Franklin Watts, 1980.
Jackson, Jesse. *Make a Joyful Noise Unto the Lord: The Life of Mahalia Jackson.* Crowell, 1974.
Jordan, June. *Who Look At Me.* Crowell, 1969; art and poetry.

Katz, William L. *Black West.* Doubleday, 1973; history.
Keats, Ezra J. *John Henry, An American Legend.* Pantheon, 1965.
King, Martin Luther. *Why We Can't Wait.* Harper, 1964.

Laye, Camara. *The Guardian of the Word.* Adventura, 1984; translation by an African writer of one of the great national epics of West Africa.
Lester, Julius. *Black Folktales.* Baron, 1969.
Lester, Julius. *To Be a Slave.* Dial, 1968; anthology of personal reminiscences.
Lewis, Samella, ed. *Black Artists on Art.* Ritchie, 1969.

Malcolm X. *The Autobiography of Malcolm X.* Grove, 1965.
McCannon, Dingda [sic]. *Peaches.* Lothrop, 1974; fiction.
McDermott, Gerald. *Anansi the Spider.* Harper, African folk tales.
Meltzer, Milton, ed. *In Their Own Words: A History of the American Negro 1619-1966.* Crowell, 1965.
Miller, Ruth. *City Rose.* McGraw-Hill, 1977; fiction.
Moody, Anne. *Coming of Age in Mississippi.* Dial, 1968.
Musgrove, Margaret. *Ashanti to Zulu.* Dial, 1976; introduction to the peoples of Africa for middle readers.

Parks, Gordon. *A Choice of Weapons.* Harper, 1966; autobiography.
Peterson, Robert. *Only the Ball was White.* Prentice-Hall, 1970; history of Negro League baseball.
Petry, Ann. *Harriet Tubman, Conductor on the Underground Railroad.* Crowell, 1965.

Quarles, Benjamin. *The Negro in the Civil War.* Little, Brown, 1953.
Quarles, Benjamin. *The Negro in the Making of America.* (Collier-McMillan, 1964.

Richards, Beah. *Black Woman Speaks and Other Poems.* Inner City Press, 1974.
Richardson, Ben. *Great Black Americans.* Crowell, 1976.

Robinson, Jackie. *Baseball Has Done It.* Lippincott, 1964; autobiography.

Russell, Ross. *Bird Lives: The High Life and Hard Times of Charles (Yardbird) Parker.* Charter House, 1973; biography.

Saunders, Doris E., ed. *The Day They Marched.* Johnson, 1963.

Schechter, Betty. *The Peaceable Revolution: The Story of Non-Violent Resistance.* Houghton, 1963.

Shaw, Arnold. *The World of Soul: Black America's Contribution to the Pop Music Scene.* Regnery, 1970.

Taylor, Mildred. *Song of the Trees.* Dial, 1975; fiction.

Taylor, Mildred. *Rolling Thunder, Hear My Cry.* Dial, 1976; fiction.

Terkel, Studs. *Giants of Jazz.* Harper, 1975.

Thomas, John L. *Slavery Attacked: The Abolitionist Crusade.* Prentice-Hall, 1964.

Thum, Marcella. *Exploring Black America: A History and a Guide.* Atheneum, 1975.

Walker, Mary. *Year of the Cafeteria.* Bobbs, 1971; fiction.

Washington, Booker T. Up From Slavery. Dodd, 1972; autobiography.

Watkins, Mel, and Jay David, eds. *To Be a Black Woman: Portraits in Fact and Fiction.* Morrow, 1970.

Wilkinson, Brenda. *Ludell.* Harper, 1975; fiction.

Wright, Richard. *Black Boy.* Harper, 1969; autobiography.

Wright, Richard. *Native Son.* Harper, 1969; fiction.

Answer Key for Worksheets

Listed here are the answers for the objective portions of the worksheets following each chapter. For non-objective questions and activities, our directive is to accept any reasonable response.

Chapter 1
Africa and the Slave Trade

I 1-a, 2-c, 3-b, 4-c, 5-a, 6-c, 7-b, 8-c, 9-a, 10-a, 11-c, 12-b.

II 1-F, 2-F, 3-T, 4-F, 5-T, 6-F, 7-F, 8-T, 9-T, 10-T, 11-F, 12-F, 13-F, 14-T, 15-F, 16-F, 17-T, 18-F, 19-T, 20-T.

Chapter 2
The Years of Slavery

I 1-prosperous, 2-permanent, 3-domestic, 4-indentured, 5-regulating, 6-concerning, 7-taunting, 8-branding, 9-independence, 10-discipline, 11-incident, 12-architects, 13-mobs, 14-majority, 15-indigo, 16-privileges, 17-overseer, 18-equality, 19-economy.

II 1-c, 2-a, 3-b, 4-a, 5-c, 6-b, 7-a, 8-c, 9-c, 10-b, 11-c, 12-c, 13-a, 14-c, 15-b.

Chapter 3
The Fight Against Slavery

I Crossword Puzzle

II 1-running away, self-mutilation, suicide, violence against masters, organized rebellions; 2-Gabriel Prosser, Denmark Vesey, Nat Turner; 3-William Lloyd Garrison, 4-Lydia Child, 5-Prudence Crandall, 6-Frederick Douglass, 7-Sojourner Truth, 8-Elijah Lovejoy, 9-Levi Coffin, 10-Harriet Tubman, Moses, 11-runaway (accept any reasonably close definition), 12-*Uncle Tom's Cabin*.

Chapter 4
Emancipated, but Not Free

IA 1-c, 2-b, 3-b, 4-b, 5-b, 6-a, 7-b, 8-c, 9-c, 10-b, 11-c, 12-b, 13-a.

II 1-I, 2-B, 3-K, 4-D, 5-J, 6-C, 7-G, 8-N, 9-A, 10-H, 11-M, 12-E, 13-F, 14-L.

Chapter 5
Looking For Solutions

IA 1-bleak, 2-allies, 3-authorities, 4-recreational, facilities; 5-discrimination, 6-founded, 7-ambition, 8-passion, 9-previously, influential; 10-participation, 11-unsanitary, 12-migration, 13-character, 14-compromise.

II 1-T, 2-F, 3-F, 4-F, 5-T, 6-F, 7-T, 8-T, 9-T, 10-F, 11-T, 12-F, 13-T, 14-F, 15-F, 16-F, 17-F, 18-T, 19-T, 20-F.

Chapter 6
An Explosion of Words and Music

I 1-composers, 2-decades, century; 3-waifs, 4-literature, tradition; 5-poverty, fashionable; 6-aggressive, 7-amplified, 8-desire, encouraged.

II 1-I, 2-D, 3-A, 4-E, 5-H, 6-G, 7-K, 8-F, 9-B, 10-J, 11-C.

Chapter 7
The Years of Protest

IA Wordsearch

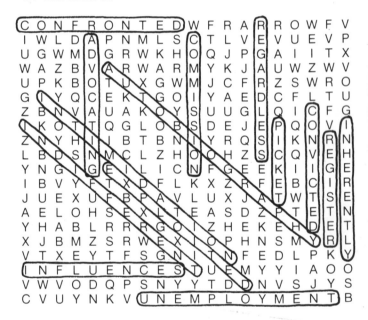

II 1-c, 2-c, 3-a, 4-b, 5-a, 6-c, 7-b, 8-a, 9-a, 10-a, 11-b, 12-b, 13-a, 14-c, 15-b, 16-b, 17-a, 18-c, 19-c, 20-b, 21-c, 22-b, 23-c, 24-b, 25-a.

Chapter 8
Freedom When?

I 1-b, 2-b, 3-a, 4-a, 5-b, 6-b, 7-a.

II 1-T, 2-F, 3-F, 4-T, 5-F, 6-F, 7-F, 8-T, 9-T, 10-F, 11-T, 12-F, 13-F, 14-T, 15-T, 16-F, 17-T.

IV 1-D, 2-I, 3-J, 4-E, 5-A, 6-H, 7-C, 8-G, 9-F, 10-B.